Junior Skill Builders

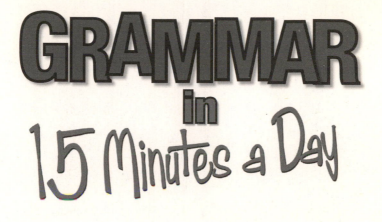

GRAMMAR in 1.5 Minutes a Day

GRAMMAR
in
15 Minutes a Day

LEARNINGEXPRESS®

NEW YORK

Library of Congress Cataloging-in-Publication Data:
Junior skill builders : grammar in 15 minutes a day.—1st ed.
    p. cm.
  ISBN: 978-1-57685-662-8
  1. English language—Grammar—Problems, exercises, etc.   2. English
language—Grammar—Examinations—Study guides.   I. LearningExpress
(Organization)
  PE1112.J86 2008
  425—dc22   2008020779

Printed in the United States of America

10 9 8 7 6 5 4 3 2 1

First Edition

For more information or to place an order, contact LearningExpress at:
    2 Rector Street
    26th Floor
    New York, NY 10006

Or visit us at:
    www.learnatest.com

C O N T E N T S

Lesson 27: Capitalization
- Understanding of capitalization of proper nouns, proper adjectives, and titles
- Review exercises of capitalization

SECTION 6: CONFUSING WORDS

Lesson 28: Troublesome Verbs
- Understanding the verbs, *lay/lie*, *sit/set*, and *did/done*
- Understanding the verbs *except/accept*, *can/may*, and *hang/hung*
- Review exercises of troublesome verbs

Lesson 29: Tricky Words
- Charts of common homonyms and homographs
- Review exercises of common homonyms and homographs

Lesson 30: Misplaced Modifiers
- Explanation and identification of dangling, squinting, and split-infinitive modifiers
- Review exercises of misplaced modifiers

Posttest

Hints for Taking Standardized Tests

Glossary

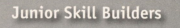

Junior Skill Builders

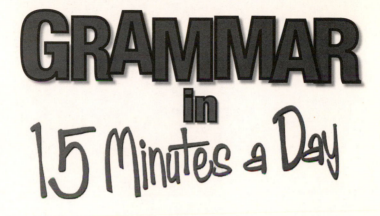

GRAMMAR
in
15 Minutes a Day

INTRODUCTION

ENGLISH IS A very complex language, but luckily there is a "users' manual" dedicated to the rules of English, referred to as grammar and usage. This is a huge set of guidelines that helps clarify the multifaceted, dynamic parts of our language (maybe you have studied many of them already at school). Understanding the inner structure of sentences and writing doesn't have to be mind numbing; it *can* be fun and challenging if you approach it with the right mindset. You will only benefit from your hard efforts to make heads or tails of English grammar and usage, and will especially reap the rewards in your writing and speaking, now and forever.

Think about how often you write—essays for school, notes and e-mails to your friends, even lists (wish lists, grocery lists, to-do lists . . . the list goes on!) These all require writing, just in different ways. Essays are more formal (*really* requiring the most of your grammar knowledge and astuteness). Other types of writing can be less formal, maybe even downright informal, and are made up of slang, emoticons, and abbreviations that would boggle the mind of any adult, but be perfectly discernible to you and your friends. *That's* the beauty and versatility of language. And as long as you understand that there is a time and place for everything, laid-back is okay . . . really. . . *adaptability* is the key. And so is having a basic, but grounded, understanding of the inner workings of English (although, trust me, *no one* expects you to be a walking grammar book). Making a determined and consistent effort to learn and apply some of the rules in this book will help you create good habits that will stay with you when it counts—like for term papers in high school and college, and letters to prospective employers when you begin job hunting in the future. These circumstances, and others, hinge on someone being able to understand and appreciate *what* you say and *how* you say it, whether your words are written or spoken.

Now, before you move on through the book, complete the grammar pretest to see what you already know and what you might need to learn, relearn, or just brush up on. Then, tackle the lessons, one by one, or on an as-needed basis. Let's get started!

PRETEST

BEFORE YOU BEGIN your grammar study, you may want to get a clearer idea of what you already know and what you want to focus more on once you begin the lessons that follow. The pretest is a simple 30-question assessment that touches on most of the major grammar concepts covered in the book. Write your answers in the book if the book belongs to you. If it doesn't, write them on a separate piece of paper so you can review and test yourself as many times as you'd like.

Check your work by looking at the answers on page 10.

PRETEST

1. (Circle) the common nouns, <u>underline</u> the proper nouns, and [box] the abstract nouns.

coffee	kindness	kitten
Florida	sadness	Lake Michigan
sorrow	toast	lipstick
peace	computer	White House
deceit	cheerfulness	jungle
test	deer	patience

2. <u>Underline</u> the antecedents / pronouns that properly agree in gender.

Karla / she	bird / they
Joseph / his	Mrs. West / she
students / they	kite / him

3. <u>Underline</u> the antecedents / pronouns that agree in number.

kids / they	everyone / they	Fred / it
fish / they	troop / it	fish / it
each / he or she	teacher / we	both / they

4. <u>Underline</u> the action verbs.

yawn	do	poke	cook
should	sleep	peel	grow
staple	would	is	jump

5. <u>Underline</u> the linking verbs.

melt	take	dance	sit
grow	prove	appear	feel
become	look	is	drive

6. [Box] the regular verbs and <u>underline</u> the irregular verbs.

justify	mow	buy	sit
play	throw	hear	pet
walk	grow	wash	hide

7. Circle the correct form of *lay* / *lie* in each sentence.

   Janice found her pillow (laying, lying) under the bed.

   The ladder has (lain, laid) broken in the garage for over a year.

   Grandpa had (laid, lain) awake before getting up to shower.

8. Circle the correct form of *sit* / *set* in each sentence.

   The dog (set, sat) patiently as Dad read the paper.

   Donna's daughter Jamie (sit, set) the table for dinner.

   (Setting, Sitting) on the porch swing to read is so enjoyable.

9. Identify the tense of the verbs that follow as present, past, future, present perfect, past perfect, future perfect, present progressive, past progressive, or future progressive.

   will swim _____   am giving _____

   had swum _____   gave _____

   swim _____   has given _____

   swims _____   will have given _____

10. Circle the common adjectives in the following sentences.

    Nathan and his best friend Kevin played a quick game of basketball.

    The cool mountains are the perfect place to hike and observe wildlife.

    Jack is excited that his birthday party is tomorrow afternoon.

11. Write the correct indefinite pronoun in front of each noun.

    ___ home   ___ hour   ___ honor

    ___ university   ___ wallet   ___ golf club

    ___ one-eyed monster ___ upperclassman ___ orange

    ___ underdog   ___ elephant   ___ clock

    ___ ugly bug   ___ yellow jacket   ___ actor

12. Change the following proper nouns into proper adjectives by crossing out and writing in what's needed.

America	England	Inca
Japan	Texas	Hawaii
France	Virginia	Denmark

13. Determine whether each boldfaced word in the sentences is a possessive
pronoun or a possessive adjective by writing in PP or PA above it.

His soda sprayed all over **his** clothes and **mine**.

We played kickball on **our** new blacktop at school.

I showed **my** little sister how to tie **her** shoes.

14. Determine whether the boldfaced word in each sentence is a demonstrative pronoun or a demonstrative adjective by writing DP or DA above it.

This is really over-the-top!

Take **this** money and buy yourself a treat.

Watch **these** carefully while they boil.

15. Circle the form of comparative or superlative adjective that best completes each sentence.

Shirley's (better, best) cake ever is her triple chocolate cake with
walnuts.

Lori's hands were (smaller, more small) than mine.

Norman was (best, better) at organizing group activities than
Joshua.

16. Circle the correct form of the comparative and superlative adverbs in the
following sentences.

Kyle was (carefuller, more careful) not to run in the hall after
getting detention.

Foodworld (more often, most often) has my favorite brand of ice
cream.

Sagar ran the (fast, faster, fastest) of all the contestants.

17. Underline the adjectives and box the adverbs in the following sentences.

The four cooks fiercely competed for the position of head chef.

Jake worked diligently on his math homework before.

Morgan was sent straight to her room for disobeying her parents.

18. <u>Underline</u> the prepositional phrases in these sentences.

We walked up the street and around the corner to get milk.

For the record, Congressman Hughes supports lowering taxes.

Up the tree and over the fence, the gray squirrel skittered nervously.

19. Rewrite each sentence so that the misplaced modifiers are properly placed.

The woman was washing the sheets with hair curlers.

_____

The sand along the shore burned my feet while walking.

_____

Tina bought a potbellied pig for her cousin they call Petunia.

_____

20. <u>Underline</u> the simple subjects and box the simple predicates.

I quickly ran toward the finish line to win the race.

Ray Charles was a excellent pianist.

The silver duct tape stuck the wall very well.

21. Identify whether the boldfaced word is a direct or an indirect object in these sentences by writing DO or IO above it.

Shane poured the **dirt** from the wheelbarrow into the hole.

Ralph gave **Jim** a curious **look** when he laughed.

The coach gave his **team** a **thumbs-up** when they defended the goal successfully.

22. Circle the verb that correctly agrees with the subject in these sentences.

The airline (fly, flies) daily from Chicago to Boston.

The friends always (watch, watches) out for one another.

Everybody (want, wants) to sit in the first row for the Guns N' Roses concert.

23. (Circle) the verb that will agree with the indefinite pronouns in these sentences.

> Anything worthwhile (take, takes) patience and time.
>
> Some (need, needs) to listen to music to relax.
>
> Others (prefers, prefer) to sit in silence and meditate.

24. Determine which pronoun best fits for proper pronoun–antecedent agreement in each sentence.

> The class took _____ time taking the history test.
>
> **a.** its   **b.** their   **c.** his or her
>
> Nobody handed _____ test in until the teacher asked.
>
> **a.** their   **b.** his or her   **c.** our
>
> Few finished early and read _____ novel until class was over.
>
> **a.** their   **b.** his or her   **c.** our

25. Correctly identify the types of phrases in the sentences below.

> *Wanting to be prepared for her recital,* Sara practices daily for an hour.
>
> **a.** participial phrase   **b.** appositive phrase   **c.** gerund phrase
>
> Sara, *who is preparing for her recital,* practices daily for an hour.
>
> **a.** participial phrase   **b.** appositive phrase   **c.** gerund phrase
>
> *Wanting to be prepared for her recital* is why Sara practices daily for an hour.
>
> **a.** participial phrase   **b.** appositive phrase   **c.** gerund phrase

26. Determine whether the group of words is an independent or a subordinate clause by writing IC or SC.

> Just to remind you _____   Have a nice day _____
>
> Try that again _____   After you left _____
>
> I love you _____   While we're at it _____

27. Identify the coordinating conjunction in each sentence and underline the word or group of words it is connecting.

> Bert wants to go swimming today, and Ronnie wants to go with him.

> We can go to the park on Sunday, or we can go today, but not tomorrow.

> I decided to go to the gym in the morning so I would have the afternoon free.

28. Identify the simple, compound, complex, and compound-complex sentence.
  a. Dinner was delicious.
  b. When the principal announced the winners, the audience clapped loudly and cheered for their classmates.
  c. When the weather warms up, we'll go to the beach and have a barbecue.
  d. Paula washed the car, and Renee dried it with towels.

29. Add punctuation where necessary in the following items.

> Timmys favorite superhero Mighty Man wears a red cape and a bright blue suit

> Didnt Mom ask you to pick up laundry detergent milk bananas sour cream and furniture polish from the grocery store

> The girls dresses were pink green and yellow taffeta with white grosgrain bows

30. Correctly place quotation marks, commas, and end marks in these sentences.

> I have never Mom exclaimed angrily seen someone so hardheaded in my life

> Carrie whispered I think that the actress forgot her lines

> To your left you will see Queen Elizabeth's throne said the tour guide

ANSWERS

1. Common nouns: coffee, test, toast, computer, deer, kitten, lipstick, jungle; proper nouns: Florida, Lake Michigan, White House; abstract nouns: sorrow, peace, deceit, kindness, sadness, cheerfulness, patience.

2. Karla/she; Joseph/his; Mrs. West/she; students/they

3. kids/they; everyone/they; fish/they; troop/it; fish/it; each/he or she; both/they

4. yawn, do, poke, cook, sleep, peel, grow, staple, jump

5. grow, prove, appear, feel, become, look, is

6. Regular verbs: justify, play, walk, wash; irregular verbs: mow, throw, grow, buy, hear, sit, pet, hide.

7. lying, lain, lain

8. sat, set, Sitting

9. will swim = future   am giving = present progressive
   had swum = past perfect   gave = past
   swim = present   has given = present perfect
   swims = present   will have given = future perfect

10. best, quick; cool, perfect; excited, birthday

11. a home   an hour   an honor
    a university   a wallet   a golf club
    a one-eyed monster   an upperclassman   an orange
    an underdog   an elephant   a clock
    an ugly bug   a yellow jacket   an actor

12. American, English, Incan, Japanese, Texan, Hawaiian, French, Virginian, Danish

13. PP = possessive pronoun, PA = possessive adjective
    His = PA, his = PA, mine = PP
    our = PA
    my = PA, her = PA

14. DP = demonstrative pronoun, DA = demonstrative adjective
    This = DP, this = DA, these = DP

15. best, smaller, better

16. more careful, most often, fastest

17. The four cooks fiercely competed for the position of head chef.
    Jake worked diligently on his math homework before .
    Morgan was sent straight to her room for disobeying her parents.

18. We walked up the street and around the corner to get milk.
    For the record, Congressman Hughes supports lowering taxes.
    Up the tree and over the fence, the gray squirrel skittered nervously.

19. (Possible answers.)

The woman with hair curlers was washing the sheets.

The sand along the shore burned my feet while I was walking.

Tina bought her cousin a potbellied pig they call Petunia.

20. I quickly $\boxed{\text{ran}}$ toward the finish line to win the race.

Ray Charles $\boxed{\text{was}}$ an excellent pianist.

The silver duct <u>tape</u> $\boxed{\text{stuck}}$ to the wall very well.

21. DO = direct object, DI = indirect object.

dirt = DO, Jim = IO, look = DO, team = IO, thumbs-up = DO

22. flies, watch, wants

23. takes, need, prefer

24. b. their, **b.** his or her, **a.** their

25. a. participial phrase, **b.** appositive phase, **c.** gerund phrase

26. IC = independent clause, SC = subordinate clause

Just to remind you = SC, Have a nice day = IC

Try that again = IC, After you left = SC

I love you = IC, While we're at it = SC

27. <u>Bert wants to go</u> swimming today, **and** <u>Ronnie wants to go</u> with him.

<u>We can go to the park on Sunday</u>, **or** <u>we can go today</u>, but not tomorrow.

<u>I decided to go to the gym in the morning</u> **so** <u>I would have the afternoon free.</u>

28. (a) simple, (b) compound-complex, (c) complex, (d) compound

29. Timmy's favorite superhero, Mighty Man, wears a red cape and a bright blue suit.

Didn't Mom ask you to pick up laundry detergent, milk, bananas, sour cream, and furniture polish from the grocery store?

The girls' dresses were pink, green, and yellow taffeta with white gros-grain bows.

30. "I have never," Mom exclaimed angrily, "seen someone so hardheaded in my life!"

Carrie whispered, "I think that the actress forgot her lines."

"To your left, you will see Queen Elizabeth's throne," said the tour guide.

ⓈⒺⒸⓉⒾⓄⓃ 1

parts of speech

WHEN WE SPEAK and write, we put words together in familiar patterns. In these patterns, called sentences, every word plays a specific and necessary role, sometimes several roles. The English language categorizes these roles into eight sections:

- **Nouns:** one of the two fundamental components of the English language, and is divided further into six special parts.
- **Pronouns:** words that take the place of a noun that must agree in three ways—*number*, *gender*, and *person*.
- **Verbs:** called the "movers and shakers" of written and spoken language, they are the second fundamental component of the English language, and are divided into three special parts. Verbs can be written in a number of different tenses.
- **Adjectives:** can add color and imagery, or be mechanical and uncomplicated, just by answering four simple questions.
- **Adverbs:** add vividness to written and spoken words in different ways than adjectives do.
- **Prepositions:** help express a relationship of time or space between certain words in a sentence.
- **Conjunctions:** connect words and phrases in three different ways—*coordinating*, *correlative*, and *subordinating*.
- **Interjections:** words that help a writer or speaker express emotion.

1

nouns

The finest language is mostly made up of simple
unimposing words.
GEORGE ELIOT (MARY ANNE EVANS), (1819–1880)
BRITISH POET

Learn what makes up one of the two fundamental parts of the English language—
the noun—and how to identify its six special components.

NOUNS ARE NAMING words. They identify people, places, or things in our world, and come in six different forms: *common, proper, concrete, abstract, collective,* and *compound*. A single noun can fall into several of these categories. Consider the word *notebook*, which is a common noun, a concrete noun, and a compound noun all at one time. Let's see why.

COMMON AND PROPER NOUNS

Markers, skateboard, cell phones, bike trail, shoelaces—these are everyday items that we call **common nouns**. They are ordinary names for people, places, or things that can be singular or plural. Look around you, what do you see? Four walls, perhaps a window or two, some furniture or books—all of these are common nouns. The nonspecific, ordinary noun *notebook* belongs as well.

Words like *Atlantic Ocean, Mardi Gras, Phoenix, SpongeBob,* and *Mercedes-Benz* are called **proper nouns**, because they name very *specific* people, places, or things. They are easy to recognize because of their capital letter, and can be either singular or plural. Be careful though! Don't fall into the trap of thinking that *every* capitalized word in a sentence is a proper noun. Remember, sentences must begin with a capital letter, too!

> *Philadelphia* cheesesteak sandwiches are famous.

Philadelphia is a **proper noun**, and happens to begin the sentence. It would be capitalized *anywhere* it appeared in the sentence.

> *Cheesesteak sandwiches* from Philadelphia are famous.

Cheesesteak sandwiches is a **common noun**, but is capitalized because it begins the sentence. It would be lowercase anywhere else in the sentence.

Unless the word *notebook* is part of a brand name, like the Chic Unique Notebook, it does not belong in this category, because proper nouns are very specific.

Notice the differences between these common and proper nouns in the chart below:

Common nouns	Proper nouns
restaurant	McDonald's
book	*Harry Potter and the Deathly Hollows*
actor	Johnny Depp
store	Abercrombie & Fitch
country	New Zealand

PRACTICE 1: COMMON AND PROPER NOUNS

Find and correct the capitalization errors in these sentences. You can check your answers against the key at the end of this lesson.

1. I was delighted to see katelyn and andrew last saturday Afternoon.

2. the spanish Test on tuesday was hard.

3. martin's Journey to mount rushmore in keystone, south dakota, was unforgettable.

4. charlie couldn't sleep because his Puppy, casper, whined all night long.

5. stephanie bought her jeans at the freehold raceway Mall with the gift card she got for christmas last December.

6. The smithsonian institute, in washington, d.c., has more than 19 museums altogether.

7. Our family plays monopoly and watches movies on new year's eve.

CONCRETE AND ABSTRACT NOUNS

Words that refer to something that physically exists are **concrete nouns**. Concrete nouns can be countable, like *soccer ball, controller, pizza, toothpick,* and *notebook,* or uncountable, like *air, oxygen, rice, milk,* and *sand*. Concrete nouns that are countable can be made plural; uncountable concrete nouns are always singular.

Abstract nouns name feelings, ideas, and characteristics, or qualities. They are concepts that cannot be seen or touched; they have no *physical* existence. Words like *tranquility, stubbornness, health,* and *curiosity* belong in this category. Abstract nouns are *usually* singular, uncountable nouns, but there are some exceptions—like *idea/ideas, noise/noises, freedom/freedoms,* and *power/powers.* Can you think of others?

TIP: Most abstract nouns end with these suffixes:

-ism	-ment	-ity	-ness	-th
nationalism	argument	personality	kindness	strength
-tion	**-age**	**-ship**	**-ance**	**-ence**
aggravation	courage	friendship	allowance	silence

PRACTICE 2: CONCRETE AND ABSTRACT NOUNS

Determine whether each word is a concrete noun or an abstract noun.

8. determination

9. quality

10. annoyance

11. flower

12. height

13. peacefulness

14. quarter

15. justice

16. celery

17. loyalty

18. paperclip

19. jar

20. government

21. bathtub

COLLECTIVE NOUNS

Have you ever heard of a *gaggle* of geese? A *troop* of kangaroos? Perhaps a *quiver* of cobras, or a *kaleidoscope* of butterflies? These are just a few of a long list of interesting terms we use to name groups of people or things, called **collective nouns**. Collective nouns can refer to a single unit, or to the individual members.

Term   team

> Single unit: The team *plays* its final game.

> Individual members: The team *must wash* their new uniforms.

Term   cast

> Single unit: The cast *is* rehearsing.

> Individual members: The cast carefully *practice* their lines.

PRACTICE 3: COLLECTIVE NOUNS

Using the word bank below, correctly match the collective noun to its corresponding noun. Check your answers with the key at the end of the chapter.

experts	buffalo	ships	money	wolves
snakes	monkeys	lions	ants	bees
sheep	cards	beavers	camels	hens
kittens	kangaroos	fish		

22. committee

23. army

24. herd

25. flock

26. pack

27. caravan

28. brood

29. litter

30. mob

31. flotilla

32. swarm

33. wad

34. lodge

35. deck

36. nest

37. tribe

38. pride

39. school

COMPOUND NOUNS

Toothpaste, fruit juice, jack-in-the-box. These words are what we call compound nouns. When we put two or more words together to create a new word, we have made a **compound noun**. These three compound nouns show the three ways a compound noun can be written: as one single word, as two or more separate words, or as a hyphenated word. Can you tell what two words make up the compound noun *notebook*? Yes, *note* and *book*.

Let's look at how some compound nouns are formed:

noun + noun	→	firefighter, police officer, ice-cream
noun + verb	→	carwash, milkshake, haircut
verb + noun	→	cookbook, cross-road, jump rope
adjective + noun	→	hotdog, black eye, blue jeans
adverb + noun	→	downtime, overtime, on-looker
adverb + verb	→	input, upswing, output

PRACTICE 4: COMPOUND NOUNS

In each item below, circle the words that can be combined to form a compound word. Check your answers with the key at the end of the chapter.

40. head   **a.** strong   **b.** ache   **c.** line   **d.** road

41. some   **a.** one   **b.** body   **c.** boy   **d.** thing

42. back   **a.** bone   **b.** door   **c.** drop   **d.** yard

43. news   **a.** deliverer   **b.** paper   **c.** flash   **d.** magazine

44. tennis   **a.** ball   **b.** court   **c.** match   **d.** award

45. flash   **a.** light   **b.** card   **c.** back   **d.** quiz

46. out   **a.** side   **b.** cast   **c.** field   **d.** house

47. paper   **a.** fall   **b.** plate   **c.** doll   **d.** ink

48. light   **a.** house   **b.** feather   **c.** weight   **d.** color

49. fish   **a.** tank   **b.** fry   **c.** gravel   **d.** light

50. book   **a.** mark   **b.** store   **c.** report   **d.** worm

ANSWERS

Practice 1: Common and Proper Nouns

1. I was delighted to see Katelyn and Andrew last Saturday afternoon.
2. The Spanish test on Tuesday was hard.
3. Martin's journey to Mount Rushmore in Keystone, South Dakota, was unforgettable.
4. Charlie couldn't sleep because his puppy, Casper, whined all night long.
5. Stephanie bought her jeans at the Freehold Raceway Mall with the gift card she got for Christmas last December.
6. The Smithsonian Institute, in Washington, D.C., has over 19 museums altogether.
7. Our family plays Monopoly and watches movies on New Year's Eve.

Practice 2: Concrete and Abstract Nouns

8. abstract
9. abstract
10. abstract
11. concrete
12. abstract
13. abstract
14. concrete
15. abstract
16. concrete
17. abstract
18. concrete
19. concrete
20. abstract
21. concrete

Practice 3: Collective Nouns

22. experts
23. ants
24. buffalo
25. sheep
26. wolves
27. camels
28. hens
29. kittens
30. kangaroos
31. ships
32. bees
33. money
34. beavers
35. cards
36. snakes
37. monkeys
38. lions
39. fish

Practice 4: Compound Nouns

40. a, b, c
41. a, b, d
42. a, b, c, d
43. b, c, d
44. a, b, c
45. a, b, c
46. a, b, c, d
47. b, c
48. a, c
49. a, b
50. a, b, c, d

pronouns

Words are the leaves of the tree of language, of which, if some fall away, a new succession takes their place.

JOHN FRENCH (1852–1925)
FRENCH MILITARY FIELD MARSHALL

Learn to identify the different categories of pronouns, words that take the place of a noun, and how we can make then agree in three ways: number, gender, and person.

A PRONOUN TAKES the place of a noun in a sentence. Without them, we would sound absurd when we speak.

Incorrect: Mrs. Milling stood at Mrs. Milling's classroom door and greeted Mrs. Milling's third-period students as Mrs. Milling's students walked into the classroom.

Correct: Mrs. Milling stood at *her* classroom door and greeted *her* third-period students as *they* walked into the classroom.

WAYS PRONOUNS HELP US

They can refer to *specific* nouns:

Tory did homework at her desk.

[The pronoun *her* refers to the proper noun *Tory* in the sentence.]

Those are the books I ordered.

[Here, the demonstrative pronoun *those* refers to the common noun *books*.]

They can refer to *nonspecific* nouns:

Does anyone understand this problem, or is everyone confused?

[*Anyone* and *everyone* are indefinite pronouns referring to whomever is being
   addressed in this sentence.]

They can *reflect back* to a subject:

Kevin brought himself a snack, just in case.

[Here, *himself* (the object of the sentence) is referring to the subject, *Kevin*.]

They can *emphasize* a noun:

To save time, Nancy decided to bake the cookies herself.

[*Herself* in this sentence emphasizes the subject *Nancy*.]

PERSONAL PRONOUNS

Personal pronouns are separated into points of view by person: first, second,
and third person. You use **first-person pronouns** when you want to include
yourself in the action: *I, me, we,* and *us.* **Second-person pronouns** involve the
person listening to or watching the action: *you.* **Third-person pronouns** include
everybody else but you: *he, she, her, him, it, they,* and *them.*

When pronouns are used as the subject of a sentence, they are in the sub-
jective case, and called **subject pronouns**.

I like broccoli.   *We* went home.   *He* is the coach.

SUBJECT PRONOUNS

	First Person	Second Person	Third Person
Singular	I	you	he, she, it
Plural	we	you	they

Personal pronouns are called **object pronouns** when they are used as the object in a sentence (the person or thing on the receiving end of the action), or in the objective case.

He likes *me*.   I offered to drive him *home*.   Listen to *them*!

OBJECT PRONOUNS

	First Person	Second Person	Third Person
Singular	me	you	him, her, it
Plural	us	you	them

TIP: Deciding which pronouns to use depends on the nouns being replaced and where they lie in the sentence. For instance:

Drew likes Heather.

In this sentence, *Drew* is the subject noun and *Heather* is the object noun. Let's replace them with the correct pronouns:

He (←male subject pronoun) likes *her* (←female object pronoun).

If we reverse the original sentence but keep the original pronouns, the substitutions become incorrect:

Heather likes Drew. → *Her* likes *he*.

To make the sentence correct, we must substitute the nouns with the correct pronoun case:

She (←female subject pronoun) likes *him* (←male object pronoun).

In order to choose the correct pronoun, you have to consider the gender of the noun (male, female, or neuter) and whether it is the doer of the action or the receiver of the action.

Christian took Jennifer birdwatching at the park. → *He* took *her* birdwatching at the park.

If we reverse the subject and object, we must replace them with the correct pronouns:

She took *him* birdwatching at the park.

Lastly, personal pronouns that show possession—*whose* something is—are in the possessive case, and are called **possessive pronouns**.

This book is *mine*.   The house on the left is *ours*.   Is that *yours?*

POSSESIVE PRONOUNS

	First Person	**Second Person**	**Third Person**
Singular	mine	yours	his, hers, its
Plural	ours	yours	theirs

Possessive pronouns are used in a sentence to show ownership:

Amanda's dog is tan. *Mine* is black.

....

TIP: Don't confuse possessive pronouns with possessive adjectives! They look very similar (*my, your, his, her, its, our,* and *their*), and also indicate ownership of something, but a possessive adjective must be followed by a noun in a sentence:

Adjective: This is *her* CD.   *Your* house is big.   *Our* class is over.
Pronoun: This CD is *mine*.   *His* is small.   *Theirs* is over, too.

....

INDEFINITE PRONOUNS

Indefinite pronouns begin with words like *any, every, some,* and *no.* They identify a nonspecific person or thing in a sentence. Some indefinite pronouns can only be singular, some can only be plural, and others can be both. Let's see.

INDEFINITE PRONOUNS

Singular: no one, nobody, nothing, anyone, anybody, anything, everyone, everybody, everything, someone, somebody, something, little, much, neither, either, each, one
Everyone loves that song!   Do you need anything?   Little is known about it.

Plural: several, few, both, many
Several took their turns already.   Both were anxious to go.   Few were left.

Both: some, any, most, all, none
All is well.   All were elated at the news.

DEMONSTRATIVE PRONOUNS

The four **demonstrative pronouns** are *this, that, these,* and *those.* They can be either a subject or an object in a sentence. We know which one to use by looking at the number of and distance of the thing(s) we are referring to.

DEMONSTRATIVE PRONOUNS

	Singular	Plural
Nearby	this	these
Far away	that	those

Examples:
What does this say?
That is too bad.
Those are pretty.
These, too.

REFLEXIVE AND INTENSIVE PRONOUNS

Reflexive and **intensive pronouns** are pronouns that end in *self* and *selves*: *myself, yourself, himself, herself, itself, ourselves, yourselves, themselves.* Reflexive pronouns are used when the subject and object are the same:

She had to drag *herself* out of bed after an awful night's sleep.

Intensive pronouns emphasize the subject of the sentence:

Hannah herself made the dinner reservations.

· ·

TIP: If you remove the intensive pronoun from a sentence, the meaning remains clear. You cannot do the same with a reflexive pronoun, or the meaning becomes distorted.

· ·

PRACTICE: PRONOUNS

In the following sentences, identify the **boldface** pronoun as *personal, possessive, demonstrative, reflexive, intensive,* or *indefinite.*

1. **Those** used to be dad's, but **they** are now **mine**. **He** gave them to **me**.

2. **It** sold out so quickly, **they themselves** were lucky to be going to the concert.

3. Jack unhitched the tractor **himself** and drove **it** to the field to do some plowing.

4. **Something** was bothering **him**, but **no one** knew what **it** was.

5. Alison thought that **these** were prettier earrings than the ones **she** saw earlier.

6. **Both** of the kittens were so cute and cuddly, **it** was hard to choose.

7. Jake walked up to the giant redwood and said, "**This** is the biggest tree **I** have ever seen."

8. **It** looks like **everybody** is going on the field trip.

9. Is this pair of jeans **yours** or **mine**?

10. Wow! **She** has a great costume! There is **no one** in class as creative as Diana.

ANSWERS

1. **Those**—demonstrative, **they**—personal, **mine**—possessive, **He**—personal, **them**—personal, **me**—personal
2. **It**—personal, **they**—personal, **themselves**—intensive
3. **himself**—reflexive, **it**—personal
4. **Something**—indefinite, **him**—personal, **no one**—indefinite, **it**—personal
5. **these**—demonstrative, **she**—personal
6. **Both**—indefinite, **it**—personal
7. **This**—demonstrative, **I**—personal
8. **It**—personal, **everybody**—indefinite
9. **yours**—possessive, **mine**—possessive
10. **She**—personal, **no one**—indefinite

verbs

Like everything metaphysical the harmony between thought and reality is to be found in the grammar of the language.

LUDWIG WITTGENSTEIN (1889–1951)
AUSTRIAN PHILOSOPHER

Verbs are the second fundamental component of English. Learn how to discern between action, linking, and helping verbs, and why they are called the movers and shakers of written and spoken language.

ACTION VERBS

Most **action verbs** are visible—the action can be seen—as in the words *skate*, *text*, *sleep*, *pick*, *grab*, *swim*, and *clap*. When we have to identify action words in sentences, it is generally pretty easy. Some, though, are more challenging to identify because they are much less obvious to our eyes. It's hard to see the action of words like *think*, *yearn*, *wish*, *believe*, *consider*, *need*, *understand*, *remember*, and *assume*. We refer to verbs like these as mental verbs, but we must remember that they, too, are doing verbs.

Visible action verbs:

I jog every afternoon.   Justin cooks very well.

Betsy fell on the sidewalk.   The audience clapped loudly.

Invisible action verbs:

I thought it was delicious.   Donna wanted to play too.

We need to be more aware.   Shawna believes everyone.

PRACTICE 1: ACTION VERBS

Identify the action verbs in the following sentences. You may check your answers with the key at the end of the lesson.

1. The clock in the living room chimed every hour.

2. You need a paperclip to secure the papers.

3. Open your book to page 15.

4. Uncle Drew cast his fishing line off the edge of the pier.

5. Lexi considered Morgan to be her best friend.

6. Marcia watched the squirrel hop from limb to limb.

7. Heather understood why.

LINKING VERBS

Linking verbs convey a state of being or condition. In a sentence, they link, or connect, a noun with an *adjective*, a word that describes the noun:

N   V ADJ   N   V   ADJ

The grapefruit *tasted* sour.   His pockets *appeared* empty.

or with another noun, used to identify the first noun:

N   V   N   N   V   N

Fred *became* the coach.   The clue *proved* to be the key.

Sometimes you will encounter a word that looks like an action verb, when it is really a linking verb. One trick to knowing the difference between the two is looking for the adjective that is describing the noun. If the adjective is not there, then you have an action verb.

Action: Lucas tasted the stew.

Lucas actually tastes the stew; therefore, *tasted* is an action verb.

Linking: The stew tasted salty.

The stew is NOT tasting anything. The adjective *salty* is describing the noun *stew*, so the verb is a linking verb.

Another trick is to replace the verb in the sentence with the verb *is*. If it makes sense, then the sentence contains a linking verb. For example,

Kevin *felt* the sandpaper.   Kevin *is* the sandpaper.

This is silly—Kevin is NOT sandpaper! *Felt* is an action verb in this sentence.

Kevin *felt* sick this morning.   Kevin *is* sick this morning.

Yes, this is sensible—*felt* in this sentence is a linking verb.

You should make yourself familiar with this list of verbs that can be both action verbs and linking verbs (remember that their tenses can vary, for example, *appear*, *appears*, and *appeared*).

VERBS THAT CAN BE ACTION VERBS AND LINKING WORDS

appear	act	become	come	fall
feel	get	grow	lie	look
prove	seem	smell	sound	taste
turned				

PRACTICE 2: LINKING VERBS

Determine whether the italicized verbs in the following sentences are action or linking verbs. You can check your answers beginning on page 34.

8. Mom's chicken and dumplings *taste* too salty for some reason.

9. Charlotte *grew* green and yellow peppers in her container garden.

10. We *turned* at the light and headed home.

11. Pop *grew* angry when we didn't listen carefully.

12. She liked to *smell* the flowers when she walked past the vase.

13. The air *smelled* stale, so we opened the window.

14. Christian and Louise *tasted* Aunt Betty's delicious peach cobbler.

15. Jodi's white socks *turned* pink in the wash.

HELPING VERBS

One last type of verb we use is the helping verb. **Helping verbs** are used to enhance a main verb's meaning by giving us more information about its tense. Do you recognize these common helping verbs?

COMMON HELPING VERBS

am	is	are	was	were	be	do	does	did
have	had	has	may	might	must	shall	will	can
should	would	could	ought					

In a sentence, a main verb can have as many as three helping verbs in front of it. For example:

Nate *served* the ball to his opponent.
Nate *will serve* the ball to his opponent.
Nate *should have served* the ball to his opponent.

When a main verb has one or more helping verbs, this is called a **verb phrase**. You should remember that a helping verb does not always have to be right next to the main verb in the sentence. This is because an adverb (*not, only,* and *-ly* words) usually separates the helping verbs. For example,

Eddie *will* surely *choose* the largest slice of pie.
Caroline *could* not *have eaten* all those cookies.

PRACTICE 3: HELPING VERBS

Identify the verb phrases in the following sentences. Then, identify the helping verbs and the main verbs. You may check your answers with the key at the end of the lesson.

16. Steven and Craig must have had permission to leave early.

17. Mitsy should vacuum the carpet before she dusts the furniture.

18. The remote control must have fallen behind the sofa cushion.

19. It was understood that the group would be meeting in the commons after school.

20. Jesse will not be going to soccer practice this afternoon.

21. Meghan might not have practiced enough for her recital.

22. The weatherman thinks it might snow tomorrow afternoon.

ANSWERS

Practice 1: Action Verbs

1. chimed
2. need
3. Open
4. cast
5. considered
6. watched, hop
7. understood

Practice 2: Linking Verbs

8. linking
9. action
10. action
11. linking
12. action
13. linking
14. action
15. linking

Practice 3: Helping Verbs

16. Verb phrase: must have had; helping verb(s): must have; main verb: had
17. Verb phrase: should vacuum; helping verb(s): should; main verb: vacuum
18. Verb phrase: must have fallen; helping verb(s): must have; main verb: fallen
19. Verb phrase: was understood; helping verb(s): was; main verb: understood
Verb phrase: would be meeting; helping verb(s): would be; main verb: meeting
20. Verb phrase: will be going; helping verb(s): will be; main verb: going
21. Verb phrase: might have practiced; helping verb(s): might have; main verb: practiced
22. Verb phrase: might snow; helping verb(s): might; main verb: snow

verb tenses

Only in grammar can you be more than perfect.
WILLIAM SAFIRE (1929–   )
AMERICAN AUTHOR

Verb tenses are used to indicate specific periods of when we are writing or speaking. We can tell when something is happening, has already happened, or has yet to happen. See and learn how it's done.

THREE BASIC VERB tenses help us understand when something is going to happen or has happened: in the present, the past, or the future. We can then subdivide those into three more categories: simple, progressive, and perfect.

	Simple	Progressive	Perfect
Present	drive	am/is/are driving	have/has driven
Past	drove	was/were driving	had driven
Future	will drive	will be driving	will have driven

Let's look at these tenses more closely. The three basic tenses we are most familiar with are the simple, progressive, and perfect.

SIMPLE

Present tense indicates present action or action that happens on a regular basis.

We *sing* the National Anthem before ball games.

Past tense indicates that the action has already happened.

He *broke* his leg skiing yesterday.

Future tense indicates that the action hasn't yet happened, but will.

They *will audition* for this year's school play.

PROGRESSIVE

Present progressive tense indicates action that is in progress. The present progressive is formed by combining *am*, *is*, *are* with the *-ing* form of the verb:

Trudy *is writing* a letter to her grandmother.

Past progressive tense indicates action that happened at some specific time in the past. The past progressive is formed by combining *was* or *were* with the *-ing* form of the verb:

George *was playing* football in the rain.

Future progressive tense indicates action that is continuous or will occur in the future. The future progressive is formed by combining *will be* with the *-ing* form of the verb:

Doreen *will be attending* her brother's wedding this summer.

PERFECT

Present perfect tense indicates that the action had started some time in the past and is ongoing into the present time. The present perfect is formed by combining the helping verbs *have* or *has* with the past participle form of the verb. The past participle is usually the simple past form of the verb (verb + *ed*); for example, *hike* becomes *hiked*, or *stop* becomes *stopped*. Sometimes, though, the verb is irregular; for example, *run* becomes *ran* (not *runned*), or *know* becomes *knew* (not *knowed*).

With regular past participle: Hannah *has cleaned* all day.
With irregular past participle: Justin *has lost* his cell phone.

Past perfect tense indicates action that occurred some time in the past before another action was begun. The past perfect is formed by combining the helping verb *had* with the past participle form of the verb.

> Luckily, Cory's flight *had left* the airport before the snowstorm hit.

Future perfect tense indicates action that will occur and finish in the future before another action has begun. The future perfect tense is formed by combining the helping verbs *will have, would have,* or *will have been* with the past participle form of the verb.

> David *will have attended* Ocean Township Intermediate School for four years before going to high school.

IRREGULAR VERBS

Most verbs are regular, which means that you can add *-ed* to the end of the word with little or no change (an occasional doubling of a final consonant might be required, or only *-d* is added to words already ending in *-e*). English also has many *irregular verbs*, which don't follow a predictable pattern like adding *-ed* to form the past tense. The conjugation of these verbs into tenses will require memorization. Let's look at the principal parts of these verbs.

SOME COMMON IRREGULAR VERBS

Past	Present	Past Participle
be	was/were	been
beat	beat	beaten
become	became	become
begin	began	begun
bite	bit	bitten
blow	blew	blown
break	broke	broken
bring	brought	brought
broadcast	broadcast	broadcast
build	built	built
buy	bought	bought
catch	caught	caught
choose	chose	chosen

SOME COMMON IRREGULAR VERBS *(Continued)*

Past	Present	Past Participle
come	came	come
cost	cost	cost
cut	cut	cut
do	did	done
draw	drew	drawn
drink	drank	drunk
drive	drove	driven
eat	ate	eaten
fall	fell	fallen
feed	fed	fed
feel	felt	felt
fight	fought	fought
find	found	found
fly	flew	flown
forbid	forbade	forbidden
forget	forgot	forgotten
forgive	forgave	forgiven
freeze	froze	frozen
get	got	gotten
give	gave	given
go	went	gone
grow	grew	grown
hang	hung	hung
have	had	had
hear	heard	heard
hide	hid	hidden
hit	hit	hit
hold	held	held
hurt	hurt	hurt
keep	kept	kept
know	knew	known
lay	laid	laid
lead	led	led
learn	learned	learned
leave	left	left
lend	lent	lent
let	let	let

SOME COMMON IRREGULAR VERBS *(Continued)*

Past	Present	Past Participle
lie	lay	lain
light	lit	lit
lose	lost	lost
make	made	made
mean	meant	meant
meet	met	met
mistake	mistook	mistaken
mow	mowed	mowed/mown
pay	paid	paid
proofread	proofread	proofread
put	put	put
quit	quit	quit
read	read	read
ride	rode	ridden
ring	rang	rung
rise	rose	risen
run	ran	run
say	said	said
see	saw	seen
seek	sought	sought
sell	sold	sold
send	sent	sent
sew	sewed	sewed/sewn
shake	shook	shaken
shave	shaved	shaved/shaven
shine	shone	shone
shoot	shot	shot
show	showed	showed/shown
shrink	shrank	shrunk
shut	shut	shut
sing	sang	sung
sink	sank	sunk
sit	sat	sat
sleep	slept	slept
slide	slid	slid
speak	spoke	spoken
speed	speeded/sped	speeded/sped

SOME COMMON IRREGULAR VERBS *(Continued)*

Past	Present	Past Participle
spend	spent	spent
spread	spread	spread
spring	sprang	sprung
stand	stood	stood
steal	stole	stolen
stick	stuck	stuck
sting	stung	stung
strike	struck	struck/stricken
strive	strove	strived/striven
swear	swore	sworn
swim	swam	swum
take	took	taken
teach	taught	taught
tear	tore	torn
tell	told	told
think	thought	thought
throw	threw	thrown
understand	understood	understood
upset	upset	upset
wake	woke	woken
wear	wore	worn
weep	wept	wept
win	won	won
wind	wound	wound
write	wrote	written

Note: All verbs have the same parts (present, past, past participle). Unlike irregular verbs, the **past participle** of regular verbs is always the past form of the verb. For example:

Past	Present	Past Participle
jog	jogged	jogged
change	changed	changed
walk	walked	walked
pick	picked	picked

PRACTICE: BASIC, PROGRESSIVE, AND PERFECT TENSES

On a piece of paper, complete the table below according to the prompt, and then check your answers at the end of the chapter on page 42.

	Basic	**Progressive**	**Perfect**
1. take	(present)	(past progressive)	(future perfect)
2. ride	(future)	(present progressive)	(present perfect)
3. speak	(past)	(future progressive)	(past perfect)
4. drift	(present)	(past progressive)	(future perfect)
5. write	(past)	(future progressive)	(present perfect)
6. swim	(future)	(present progressive)	(future perfect)
7. stop	(past)	(past progressive)	(past perfect)
8. eat	(present)	(future progressive)	(future perfect)
9. sing	(past)	(present progressive)	(past perfect)
10. fly	(future)	(past progressive)	(future perfect)

Make the necessary changes to the boldfaced verbs in each sentence. You can check your answers on the following page.

11. Aunt Penny **will began** her workshop on watercolor painting at 3 P.M.

12. Mrs. West **spend** the weekend in New York City with her daughter.

13. While I **nap** yesterday afternoon, the sun **shine** brightly through the window.

14. Jason **throwed** the stick for his dog Gatsby to catch.

15. Watched the game from the stands, Mike **cheering** for the home team.

ANSWERS

	Basic	Progressive	Perfect
1. take	(take, takes)	(was/were taking)	(will have taken)
2. ride	(will ride)	(is/am riding)	(has ridden)
3. speak	(spoke)	(will be speaking)	(had spoken)
4. drift	(drift, drifts)	(was/were drifting)	(will have drifted)
5. write	(wrote)	(will be writing)	(has written)
6. swim	(will swim)	(is/am swimming)	(will have swum)
7. stop	(stopped)	(was/were stopping)	(had stopped)
8. eat	(eat, eats)	(will be eating)	(will have eaten)
9. sing	(sang)	(is/am singing)	(had sung)
10. fly	(will fly)	(was/were flying)	(will have flown)

A variety of correct answers are provided for item numbers 11–15.

11. Aunt Penny **will begin** her workshop on watercolor painting at 3 P.M.
    Aunt Penny **began** her workshop on watercolor painting at 3 P.M.
    Aunt Penny **will have begun** her workshop on watercolor painting at 3 P.M.
12. Mrs. West **spent** the weekend in New York City with her daughter.
    Mrs. West **will spend** the weekend in New York City with her daughter.
    Mrs. West **had spent** the weekend in New York City with her daughter.
    Mrs. West **has spent** the weekend in New York City with her daughter.
13. While I **napped** yesterday afternoon, the sun **shone** brightly through the window.
14. Jason **threw** the stick for his dog Gatsby to catch.
    Jason **throws** the stick for his dog Gatsby to catch.
    Jason **will throw** the stick for his dog Gatsby to catch.
    Jason **had thrown** the stick for his dog Gatsby to catch.
    Jason **has thrown** the stick for his dog Gatsby to catch.
15. **Watching** the game from the stands, Mike **cheered** for the home team.
    Watching the game from the stands, Mike **was cheering** for the home team.
    Watching the game from the stands, Mike **has cheered** for the home team.
    Watching the game from the stands, Mike **had cheered** for the home team.
    Watching the game from the stands, Mike **will cheer** for the home team.
    Watching the game from the stands, Mike **will be cheering** for the home team.

adjectives

*. . . often when I write I am trying to make words do the work of
line and colour. I have the painter's sensitivity to light. Much (and
perhaps the best) of my writing is verbal painting.*

ELIZABETH BOWEN (1899–1973)
IRISH NOVELIST

Some adjectives add color and imagery to our writing and speech, while others
are very mechanical and uncomplicated. Learn how and when to use all kinds of
adjectives.

ADJECTIVES ARE MODIFIERS that describe or provide more specific information about nouns and pronouns. If a teacher asked a group of students to picture an *elephant* in their minds, one student might have a mental image of a big
gray elephant; another might be imagining the cute, fluffy, stuffed one sitting
on her shelf at home. This is because the word *elephant* is too broad and non-
descript. If common adjectives, everyday descriptors such as *big, gigantic, white,
pink polka-dotted,* or *hairy* had been added, the students' mental images would
have been more aligned to that of the teacher.

All adjectives answer three specific questions about the nouns or pronouns they are modifying: *what kind? (horizontal, strong, critical), which one(s)?
(the, this, that, these, those),* and *how many? (eight, few, countless, several).* While
adjectives often come before the nouns they're modifying, they can come afterward, too:

Fred, exhausted and frustrated, took a minute to gather his thoughts
before forging ahead.

ARTICLES

The three words *a*, *an*, and *the* are special adjectives that we call **articles**. *The* is a definite article, which implies something specific—pick *the* card; not just any card. *A* and *an* are indefinite articles, which are nonspecific—pick *a* card; *any* card.

Deciding which indefinite article to place in front of a word depends upon the initial sound of the word, not the first letter of the word. The article *an* should be placed before words that begin with a vowel sound. *A* is placed before words that begin with consonant sounds. For instance, the word *honest* begins with the consonant *h*, but since it begins with a short *o* vowel sound (the *h* is silent), it takes the article *an*. The word *house*, on the other hand, takes the article *a*: It also begins with an *h*, but the consonant sound (*h*) is pronounced. Don't let the initial letter of the word fool you! Be careful of words like *one*, *unicorn*, and *honest*.

PROPER ADJECTIVES

We distinguish proper nouns, like *Nathan*, *Mount Everest*, and *Colorado*, from common nouns, like *guy*, *mountain*, and *state*, by capitalizing them. **Proper adjectives** are proper nouns acting like adjectives because they are modifying a noun or pronoun. *Xerox copier*, *New York skyline*, and *Japanese food* begin with proper adjectives, each answering the question *what kind?* or *which one?* about the noun following it.

What kind of copier?	Xerox
Which skyline?	New York
What kind of food?	Japanese

POSSESSIVE ADJECTIVES

Possessive adjectives look very similar to the possessive pronouns you learned about in Lesson 2. Like possessive pronouns, the possessive adjectives—*my, your, his, her, its, our, their*—express possession. What distinguishes one from the other is that a possessive adjective must be followed by a noun. Possessive adjectives answer *which one?* about the noun they are modifying.

Adjective:	*My* slippers are here.	*Our* pool is heated.
Pronoun:	*Yours* are over there.	*Theirs* is not.

DEMONSTRATIVE ADJECTIVES

Demonstrative adjectives—*this, that, these, those*—also answer *which one?* about the noun they are modifying, and must also come before the noun being modified.

> *that* kite   *this* phone   *these* tickets   *those* blankets

Like possessive adjectives, if the words *this, that, these, those* are not followed by a noun, they are considered pronouns. For example:

> *This* is stale.   *That* took forever.   *These* are confusing.   *Those* fell out.

PRACTICE: ADJECTIVES

Identify the type of adjective (boldfaced) in each of these sentences.

1. Margaret wore **these silver** sandals with **her new** dress.

2. That is **an interesting** question, Alex.

3. Nathan carried **his Gibson** guitar and **Bose** amp to **the** car.

4. My new pocket watch had stopped ticking.

5. Last night, **our white Persian** cat, Snowball, was **scared**, and he hid under **my** bed.

Correctly place the indefinite articles *a* or *an* in front of each of these words.

6. ___ hourglass

7. ___ octopus

8. ___ university

9. ___ youth group

10. ___ excellent bargain

11. ___ upstanding citizen

12. ___ honorable man

13. ___ unopened box

14. ___ unique find

15. ___ one-way street

Identify whether the boldfaced word is a proper noun or a proper adjective.

16. Most of the **Canadian** border is made up of the forty-ninth parallel.

17. My mother's favorite flower is the **African** violet.

18. **Thai** is a difficult language to learn.

19. The orange juice is made from **Florida** oranges.

20. This **Thanksgiving** we will travel to Massachusetts.

Determine whether the boldfaced word is a possessive adjective or a possessive pronoun.

21. **Its** Greek salad is a popular menu selection.

22. **His** name is Jeffrey.

23. **My** dad thought the key was **his**, but was mistaken.

24. **Their** bungalow was just down the walkway from **ours**.

25. **Your** eyes should be checked if **this** is difficult to read.

Determine whether the boldfaced word in the sentence is a demonstrative adjective or a demonstrative pronoun.

26. This day was absolutely the worst!

27. Those antique tea cups must be very fragile.

28. These have got to be the best garlic knots I've ever tasted.

29. That doesn't make a good argument, no matter how you put it.

30. Charlotte chose **that** one on the right.

ANSWERS

1. **these**: demonstrative; **silver**: common; **her**: possessive; **new**: common
2. **an**: indefinite article; **interesting**: common
3. **his**: possessive; **Gibson**: proper; **Bose**: proper; **the**: definite article
4. **My**: possessive; **new**: common; **pocket**: common
5. **our**: possessive; **white**: common; **Persian**: proper; **scared**: common; **my**: possessive
6. **an** hourglass
7. **an** octopus
8. **a** university
9. **a** youth group
10. **an** excellent bargain
11. **an** upstanding citizen
12. **an** honorable man
13. **an** unopened box
14. **a** unique find
15. **a** one-way street
16. proper adjective
17. proper adjective
18. proper noun
19. proper adjective
20. proper noun
21. **Its**: possessive adjective
22. **His**: possessive adjective

23. My: possessive adjective; **his**: possessive pronoun

24. Their: possessive adjective; **ours**: possessive pronoun

25. Your: possessive adjective; **this**: possessive pronoun

26. This: demonstrative adjective

27. Those: demonstrative adjective

28. These: demonstrative pronoun

29. That: demonstrative pronoun

30. that: demonstrative adjective

adverbs

Grammar, which rules even kings . . .
MOLIERE (1622–1673)
FRENCH PLAYWRIGHT

Adverbs add vividness and imagery to language in a different way than adjectives do. Learn these differences, and how you can apply them to your writing and speech.

LIKE ADJECTIVES, ADVERBS are also modifiers. They modify verbs most often, but they can also modify adjectives and other adverbs. Some adverbs are very easy to spot, like the words *so, very,* and *really,* and most *-ly* words.

Adverbs answer four specific questions about the verbs, adjectives, and adverbs they modify: *where?* (*everywhere, outside, under*), *when?* (*always, yesterday, later*), *how?* (*quickly, voraciously, surprisingly*), and *to what extent?* (*so, very, really*). Like adjectives, some adverbs can come either before or after the words they're modifying:

Kathi and Fred walked *briskly* around the track.

Kathi and Fred *briskly* walked around the track.

TIP: While spotting -*ly* adverbs can be fairly simple, it's important to keep in mind that not all -*ly* words are adverbs. Some can be adjectives: *friendly*, *neighborly*, *yearly*, *mannerly*, *daily*, *lovely*, *elderly*, and *cowardly*, to name just a few. Remember to look for the type of word the -*ly* word is modifying: It's an adjective if it modifies a noun or a pronoun; it's an adverb if it modifies a verb, an adjective, or another adverb.

The following chart provides you with some examples of how adverbs are used. As you look through the chart, see if you can identify what question the adverb is answering about the modified word.

WORDS AN ADVERB CAN MODIFY

Verbs	Julie can *hardly* **wait** for school to end.	Melissa **turned** *around*.
	They **traveled** *far* and *wide*.	**Go** *quickly* and tell her to **come** *here*.
Adjectives	Scott looked *rather* **surprised**.	You're *so* **helpful**, thank you.
	The soup was *too* **hot** to eat.	Brrr! It's *quite* **chilly** now.
Adverbs	Sara danced *extremely* **well** this year.	Greg came *unusually* **late**.
	The car was following *too* **closely**.	He *almost* **never** complains.

DISTINGUISHING BETWEEN ADVERBS AND ADJECTIVES

Sometimes we see a word used one way in a sentence, and the very same word used in a completely different way in another sentence. How can that be? Simple! Just as you might be a son or daughter to your parents, a brother or sister to your siblings, and a grandson or granddaughter to your grandparents, a word can also wear different hats from sentence to sentence. For instance:

Stacy commented that the *test* was **harder** than she thought.

Hal should *try* **harder** to be patient with his younger sister.

In the first sentence, *harder* modifies the noun *test*, making it an adjective. It is answering *what kind* of test it was. In the second sentence, *harder* is modifying the verb *try*, answering *how* Hal should try.

The chart on the opposite page illustrates some other adverbs and adjectives that share the same form.

SOME ADVERBS AND ADJECTIVES THAT SHARE THE SAME FORM

Adjective	Adverb
The **fast** car crossed the finish line.	He fell **fast** asleep.
The **early** class filled up quickly.	We got home **early** from school.
The wall was too **high** blocked the view.	Kyle jumped **high** to reach the shelf.
Some others are near, late, far, straight, hard, long, low, right, wrong, wide, little, daily, weekly, monthly, and yearly.	

On the other end of the spectrum, some adjectives and adverbs that look similar are not interchangeable. You can avoid the trap by learning their differences.

Good and Well

The word *good* is only an adjective, never an adverb. *Good* implies *acceptable* or *satisfactory*.

Ian is a *good* diver.

Well can be an adjective or an adverb. As an adjective, *well* means *healthy*:

Veronica didn't look *well* when I saw her.

The adverb form signifies how something is done:

He played his defensive position *well* this season.

Bad and Badly

Bad is also only an adjective, never an adverb. It signifies how someone looks, feels, sounds, or just is (in any form of the verb *be*):

Sandy's broken toe looked *bad*.

Badly is only an adverb, never an adjective. It modifies the action verb in the sentence, telling how something is done:

She limped *badly* for more than two weeks.

PRACTICE: ADVERBS

Identify common adverbs in the following sentences. You can check your answers on the following page.

1. In his bathrobe, John stepped outside to quickly retrieve the morning paper.

2. It was an uncommonly warm April day; one too nice to stay inside.

3. The sun was shining brightly, and there wasn't a single cloud in the sky.

4. Immediately, John decided that it was the perfect day for a picnic.

5. He went right up the stairs to wake up his family and get dressed.

6. Unfortunately, his wife, Ann, could not go. She already had plans to meet with her friends for coffee later.

7. Mark, his teenage son, grumbled loudly and hastily buried his head under his pillow, lamenting the thought of having to roll out of bed before noon.

8. John, hardly discouraged, headed over to the park for a jog, still looking forward to enjoying the warm spring weather.

Determine whether the boldfaced words in the sentences are adjectives or adverbs. You can check your answers on the opposite page.

9. The **past** school year has been productive in many ways.

10. I searched **far** and **wide** to find the perfect shade of blue for my living room walls.

11. He said the **right** answer; I misunderstood, and said the **wrong** one.

12. Turn **right** at the light and make a left into the **wide** driveway.

13. Please don't walk too **fast**.

14. I had to open the door **wide** to get the package inside.

15. The **fast** car zoomed **past** the spectators as it headed for the finish line.

ANSWERS

1. outside, quickly
2. uncommonly, too, inside
3. brightly
4. Immediately
5. right, up
6. already, later
7. loudly, hastily
8. hardly, over, still, forward
9. adjective
10. adverb, adverb
11. adjective, adjective
12. adverb, adjective
13. adverb
14. adverb
15. adjective, adverb

comparative adjectives and adverbs

The English language is nobody's special property.
It is the property of the imagination:
it is the property of the language itself.

DEREK WALCOTT (1930–)
PLAYWRIGHT

There is one more way in which adjectives and adverbs are used: to compare one thing to another in relation to varying amounts—more, most, less, and least.

WE CAN USE adjectives and adverbs to show comparison of things and actions in our writing and speaking. We have three levels or degrees of comparison for both: **positive**, **comparative**, and **superlative**.

The positive degree represents the base form of the adjective or adverb:

ADJ: Her sweater is *white*.   ADV: He walks *fast*.

In the comparative degree, a comparison between two things or actions is made:

ADJ: Her sweater is *whiter* than mine.   ADV: He walks *faster* than I do.

In the superlative degree, a comparison between more than two things or actions is made:

ADJ: Her sweater is the *whitest*.   ADV: He walks the *fastest*.

RULES TO REMEMBER

Rule 1: Many adjectives and adverbs use *-er* and *-est* endings.

Adjectives	Adverbs
large, larger, largest	hard, harder, hardest
cold, colder, coldest	early, earlier, earliest

However, we can't say *good, gooder, goodest,* or *much, mucher, muchest.* Such adjectives and adverbs are called **irregular**. Their comparative and superlative forms have to be memorized. Here are some words that fall into this category.

(adj) good, better, best	(adj) bad, worse, worst
(adv) well, better, best	(adv) badly, worse, worst
(both) much, more, most	(both) little, less, least
(both) far, farther, farthest	(both) far, further, furthest

Rule 2: Many adjectives and all adverbs that contain two or more syllables must use *more* and *most* to enhance their degree, and *less* and *least* to decrease the degree.

(two-syllable)	ADJ	careful	more careful less careful	most careful least careful
	ADV	often	more often less often	most often least often
(three-syllable)	ADJ	serious	more serious less serious	most serious least serious
	ADV	precisely	more precisely less precisely	most precisely least precisely
(four-syllable)	ADJ	intelligent	more intelligent less intelligent	most intelligent least intelligent
	ADV	successfull	more successfully less successfully	most successfully least successfully

Some adjectives that don't fit this rule are *narrow, picky, silly, clever, friendly, simple, quiet,* and *gentle.*

Rule 3: Some adjectives are called absolute adjectives or incomparable adjectives because they are words that absolutely cannot be compared, no matter how hard you try.

Take the adjective *round* for instance. What could be *rounder* than *round*? Or what could be more *perfect* than *perfect*? Get it? Other absolute adjectives are *favorite, true, false, unique, square, free,* and *complete.*

Absolute adverbs are in the same boat. Words like *all, every, completely,* and *entirely* already mean everything possible, don't they? So how could they be intensified any more than they already are? Likewise, *never* and *always,* words that express the two most extreme points of time, could hardly be stretched beyond their boundaries.

PRACTICE: COMPARATIVE ADJECTIVES AND ADVERBS

Determine which form of comparative or superlative adjective or adverb best completes each sentence. You may check your answers at the end of the lesson.

1. Mike worked (harder, more hard) at his studies this marking period; his (most low, lowest) spelling score was only a 94.

2. Monday's weather is supposed to be (hot, hotter) than yesterday's.

3. Shelby is (more good, better) at crossword puzzles than I am.

4. Raj arrived at the movie theater (earlier, earliest) than Derek, so he bought the tickets.

5. Hannah's backyard is (larger, more large) than mine.

6. JoAnn swam the (fastest, most fast) in the race.

7. Tham is the (precisest, most precise) with his calculations.

8. The (best, more better) price offered in the catalog was $9.99.

9. This glass of iced tea is (sweeter, sweetest) than the other one.

10. The youngster walked (more carefully, more careful) down the steps.

ANSWERS

1. harder, lowest
2. hotter
3. better
4. earlier
5. larger
6. fastest
7. most precise
8. best
9. sweeter
10. more carefully

prepositions and prepositional phrases

From now on, ending a sentence with a preposition is something up with which I will not put.
WINSTON CHURCHILL (1874–1965)
BRITISH STATESMAN

You'd be surprised by the number of OOPs we find in sentences. First, you will learn what OOPs actually are and then you'll learn how and where to find them.

COMMON PREPOSITIONS

about	above	across	after	against	along
among	around	as	at	before	behind
below	beneath	beside	between	beyond	but
by	concerning	despite	down	during	except
for	from	in	into	like	near
next	of	off	on	onto	out
outside	over	past	since	through	throughout
to	toward	under	underneath	unlike	until
under	up	upon	with	within	without

A **preposition** is a word that expresses a relationship between some words in a sentence, usually in regard to time (when) or space (where), much like an adverb. In order for a word to be considered a preposition, it must be part of a

prepositional phrase—a group of words, that begins with a preposition and ends with a noun or a pronoun. The noun or pronoun at the end of the phrase is called the **object of the preposition**, or OOP. Here are a few prepositional phrases:

> *across* the street
> *over* the top
> *beyond* her comprehension
> *around* the corner

Since adverbs also tell *where* and *when* about words, telling the difference between a preposition and an adverb can be tricky. Just remember that a preposition must always be part of a prepositional phrase, and in fact must always be the first word in the phrase. If it does not begin a phrase, it is an adverb. For example, the words *underneath* and *around* in the following sentences are adverbs, because they do not begin a prepositional phrase:

> I lifted the log carefully, looked *underneath*, and saw a centipede.
> When Julie heard a strange noise, she turned *around*.

Notice how the words *underneath* and *around* stand by themselves in the sentences. Adverbs can do that.

In the next two sentences, *underneath* and *around* are prepositions. Each is followed by an OOP, making a prepositional phrase:

> Sally found her mother's slippers *underneath the bed*.
> Ken looked *around the corner* before proceeding.

PRACTICE: PREPOSITIONAL PHRASES

Indicate the prepositional phrases in these sentences. You can check your answers on page 62.

1. After school, the boys played a game of baseball at the park.

2. We hid our canoe in the bushes and set up camp by the river.

3. Candy signed her name on the line and passed the paper across the table.

4. Without any warning, the dog dashed to the door and barked loudly.

5. The storm caused the tree in our front yard to fall against the house.

Try to determine whether the boldfaced word is a preposition or an adverb. You can check your answers on the following page.

6. Pull **up** a chair and sit **down by** Steven.

7. Throughout the day, Carla hummed a favorite song **to** herself.

8. Please bring the newspaper **inside**.

9. After brushing her teeth, Margaret likes to read **in** bed **before** going to sleep.

10. Run **to** the store **across** the street and pick **up** a gallon **of** milk, please.

11. Haley rode her bike **across** the bridge **into** Red Bank and hung out **with** her friends.

12. Linda stood **up** and clapped loudly.

13. Lisa borrowed a sweatshirt **from** her friend.

14. Be careful walking **across** the wet floor.

15. I saw an interesting show **about** Mt. Everest **on** television **yesterday**.

ANSWERS

1. **After school**, the boys played a game **of baseball at the park**.
2. We hid our canoe **in the bushes** and set up camp **by the river**.
3. Candy signed her name **on the line** and passed the paper **across the table**.
4. **Without any warning**, the dog dashed **to the door** and barked loudly.
5. The storm caused the tree **in our front yard** to fall **against the house**.
6. **up**: adverb; **down**: adverb; **by**: preposition
7. **Throughout**: preposition; **to**: preposition
8. **inside**: adverb
9. **After**: preposition; **in**: preposition; **before**: preposition
10. **to**: preposition; **across**: preposition; **up**: adverb; **of**: preposition
11. **across**: preposition; **into**: preposition; **with**: preposition
12. **up**: adverb
13. **from**: preposition
14. **across**: preposition
15. **about**: preposition; **on**: preposition; **yesterday**: adverb

conjunctions

When I hear the hypercritical quarreling about grammar and style, the position of the particles, etc., etc., stretching or contracting every speaker to certain rules of theirs. I see that they forget that the first requisite and rule is that expression shall be vital and natural, as much as the voice of a brute or an interjection: first of all, mother tongue; and last of all, artificial or father tongue. Essentially your truest poetic sentence is as free and lawless as a lamb's bleat.

HENRY DAVID THOREAU (1817–1862)
AMERICAN PHILOSOPHER AND POET

Coordinating, correlative, and subordinating conjunctions are tools that help us connect items in a sentence. In this lesson, you'll learn why these connectors are such essential language components.

CONJUNCTIONS CONNECT WORDS, phrases, and sentences in our writing and speech. Two common forms of conjunctions are **coordinating** and **correlative conjunctions**. While both of these connect elements that are similar in form (nouns with nouns, phrases with phrases, and sentences with sentences), the correlative conjunctions also show relationship between sentence elements and ideas. Another type of conjunction, and probably the most widely used, is the **subordinating conjunction**, which connects independent clauses (simple sentences) with subordinate clauses (a group of words that has a subject and verb like a sentence, but cannot stand by itself) that are similar in their relationship rather than in their form. Let's look at these more closely.

COORDINATING CONJUNCTIONS

The acronym FANBOYS will help you remember the seven **coordinating conjunctions** *for, and, nor, but, or, yet,* and *so.* The following chart explains what each conjunction means, and gives an example of how it can be used in a sentence.

COORDINATING CONJUNCTIONS

for	is almost like *because* or *since*; it introduces, in a formal tone, a reason
	Keith did poorly on his math test *for* he forgot to study last night.
	[sentence + sentence]
and	joins elements that are sequential and equal in importance
	The barn was up the road *and* by the river.
	[prepositional phrase + prepositional phrase]
nor	presents an alternate negative idea or thought
	Brian did not like singing, *nor* did he like dancing.
but	implies difference, contrast, and exceptions
	Our car is old *but* reliable.
	[adjective + adjective]
or	implies that an alternative or option will follow
	I can't decide if I want an apple *or* a banana with my yogurt.
	[noun + noun]
yet	implies that a contrary but logical idea will follow
	Jackie is a quiet *yet* very outgoing girl.
	[adjective + adjective]
so	suggests that a consequence will follow
	Linda turned the light on *so* she could see where she was walking.
	[sentence + sentence]

CORRELATIVE CONJUNCTIONS

Like coordinating conjunctions, **correlative conjunctions** connect elements that are similar in form. The following chart shows the five common pairs of correlative conjunctions, with examples of how they can be used in a sentence.

CORRELATIVE CONJUNCTIONS

both . . . and	*Both* popcorn *and* peanuts are popular snacks at sporting events. [noun + noun]
either . . . or	*Either* I will have to tell Lionel *or* you will. [sentence + sentence]
neither . . . nor	Zack could *neither* talk on the phone *nor* watch television the entire week. [sentence + sentence]
not only . . . but also	Maria *not only* skis *but also* snowboards. [noun + noun]
whether . . . or	Do you know *whether* Luke *or* Robin are coming to dinner? [noun + noun]

SUBORDINATING CONJUNCTIONS

Subordinating conjunctions join an independent clause (a simple sentence) with a subordinate clause (a group of words that has a subject and verb like a sentence, but cannot stand by itself). For example:

I.C. → I went to see a doctor.   S.C. → *because* my throat hurt.

We can understand the first clause, *I went to see a doctor* without any further explanation, because it is a simple sentence. But the phrase *because my throat hurt* is a subordinate clause (it begins with the subordinating conjunction *because*) and is an incomplete thought, so it must be joined with an independent clause in order to make sense. The subordinating conjunctions found at the beginning of subordinating clauses imply these four categories: time, cause and effect, condition, and contrast.

COMMON SUBORDINATING CONJUNCTIONS

Time	Cause/Effect	Condition	Contrast
after	because	as long as	although
before	so	unless	even though
when	now that	provided that	though
since	in order that	so long as	whereas
until	as if	if	even if
as soon as	whether	while	whenever

Choosing the appropriate subordinating conjunction depends on what you want to imply in your sentence. For example:

if	*If* my throat hurts, I will go to the doctor.
when	*When* my throat hurts, I will go to the doctor.
as long as	*As long as* my throat hurts, I will go to the doctor.
now that	*Now that* my throat hurts, I will go to the doctor.
before	*Before* my throat hurts, I will go to the doctor.

When using the following conjunctions, you should add *not* to the subordinate clause to imply contrast:

although	*Although* my throat hurts, I will not go to the doctor.
even though	*Even though* my throat hurts, I will not go to the doctor.

or leave them as is . . .

although	*Although* it is fall, the day is still warm.
even though	*Even though* it is fall, the day is still warm.

PRACTICE: CONJUNCTIONS

Supply the appropriate coordinating or correlative conjunctions from the chart below for the following sentences.

Coordinating	Correlative
and, or, for, nor, but,	both . . . and
yet, so	either . . . or
	whether . . . or
	neither . . . nor
	not only . . . but also

1. Kim _____ Sara played tennis.

2. _____ Jack _____ Jill went up the hill.

3. Should I order soup _____ salad with dinner?

4. Vincent moved slowly _____ steadily through the crowded room.

5. _____ did Haley arrive early, _____ she was _____ the first one there.

6. Greg wants to be either a cowboy _____ a ghost for Halloween.

7. It rained heavily, _____ the tennis match was canceled.

8. _____ you choose yellow _____ he chose blue is not the issue.

9. _____ your mother _____ your grandmother has heard you play the piano yet.

10. Write down the phone number _____ you may forget it later.

Create new sentences with the following independent clauses (simple sentences) and a sensible subordinating conjunction. Use the chart of subordinating conjunctions below to help you. (Don't forget to add punctuation so your new sentence is not a run-on.)

COMMON SUBORDINATING CONJUNCTIONS

Time	Cause/Effect	Condition	Contrast
after	because	as long as	although
before	so	unless	even though
when	now that	provided that	though
since	in order that	so long as	whereas
until	as if	if	even if
as soon as	whether	while	whenever

11. It is raining today. You should bring an umbrella along.

12. The grass needs mowing again. It was mowed on Tuesday.

13. We should arrive at the airport on time. We left a little late.

14. You may play outside. Your homework is finished.

15. We can stay at the mall. It closes.

ANSWERS

1. and

2. Both, and

3. or

4. yet

5. Not only, but, also

6. or

7. so

8. Whether, or

9. Neither, nor

10. for

11. It is raining today, **so** you should bring an umbrella along.

Since it is raining today, you should bring an umbrella along.

Because it is raining today, you should bring an umbrella along.

You should bring an umbrella along **since** it is raining today.

You should bring an umbrella along **because** it is raining today.

12. The grass needs mowing **even though** it was mowed on Tuesday.

The grass needs mowing **since** it was mowed on Tuesday.

The grass needs mowing again, **since** it was mowed on Tuesday.

Even though it was mowed on Tuesday, the grass needs mowing.

Since it was mowed on Tuesday, the grass doesn't need mowing.

13. We should arrive at the airport on time **even though** we left a little late.

We should arrive at the airport on time **although** we left a little late.

Although we left a little late, we should arrive at the airport on time.

Even though we left a little late, we should arrive at the airport on time.

14. You may play outside **provided that** your homework is finished.

You may play outside, **as long as** your homework is finished.

You may play outside, **so long as** your homework is finished.

You may play outside **now that** your homework is finished.

You may play outside **when** your homework is finished.

You may play outside **after** your homework is finished.

You may play outside **since** your homework is finished.

You may play outside **if** your homework is finished.

You may play outside **whenever** your homework is finished.

Provided that your homework is finished, you may play outside.

As long as your homework is finished, you may play outside.

So long as your homework is finished, you may play outside.

Now that your homework is finished, you may play outside.

When your homework is finished, you may play outside.

After your homework is finished, you may play outside.

Since your homework is finished, you may play outside.

If your homework is finished, you may play outside.

Whenever your homework is finished, you may play outside.

15. Until it closes, we can stay at the mall.

We can stay at the mall **until** it closes.

S E C T I O N 2

parts of a sentence

The eight parts of speech can be found within a sentence, but the parts of a sentence (subject, predicate, direct object, and indirect object) do not necessarily directly correspond with the parts of speech. For instance, the subject in a sentence can be a noun, a pronoun, a phrase, or a clause. Construction of a good sentence is essential for basic communication. In this section, you will learn how these components come together to do just that.

- **Subject:** one of the two fundamental components of the basic sentence, subjects tell the listener and the reader *whom* or *what* the sentence is about.
- **Predicate:** as the second fundamental component of a sentence, the predicate tells the reader or listener about the *condition* of the subject, or the *action* the subject is performing.
- **Direct object:** as one of two "complements," the direct object receives the action from the action verb of the sentence, and answers *whom* or *what* about that action verb.
- **Indirect object:** these depend on the direct object for existence, and tell the reader or listener *to or for whom* or *to or for what* the direct object is given or performed.

subjects and predicates

Grasp the subject, the words will follow.
CATO THE ELDER (234 B.C.–149 B.C.)
ROMAN ORATOR AND POLITICIAN

In this lesson, you will learn to identify the most basic parts of a sentence, looking at simple and complete subjects and predicates.

SENTENCES ARE THE most necessary element of speaking and writing; they allow us to communicate with others. A basic sentence can be divided up into two major components: the **complete subject**, which includes *whom* or *what* the sentence is about, and all words related to the subject; and the **complete predicate**, which includes what the subject is doing or what condition the subject is in, and all the words related to the predicate. Within the complete subject and predicate are the simple subject—one or more nouns or pronouns, and the simple predicate—one or more verbs.

SIMPLE SUBJECTS

Finding the **simple subject** of a sentence is, well, simple. You just need to ask *who?* or *what?* about the verb. For example:

S V
Gina likes lasagna.

Who likes [lasagna]? *Gina*; thus, she is the subject.
A subject can also be a common noun:

S   V
Our town has a Memorial Day parade each year.

What has [a Memorial Day parade]? The *town*; thus, it is the subject.
A subject can also be a pronoun:

S V
We listened to the radio at the beach.

Who listened [to the radio]? *We* did; thus, it is the subject.
There can also be more than one subject in a sentence:

S   S   V
Sausage and mushrooms are Leo's favorite pizza toppings.

What are [Leo's favorite pizza toppings]? *Sausage* and *mushrooms* are the subjects.
When two subjects share the same verb, this is called a **compound subject**.

....

TIP: Usually the subject of a sentence is found at the beginning of the sentence, but it can also be found in the middle or at the end of a sentence:

S   V
In the middle: Early yesterday afternoon, Janet completed the scarf she was knitting.

V   S
At the end: Hiding in the bushes was Drew's lost cat, Bootsy.

....

TRICKY SUBJECTS

Sometimes you might see a sentence that doesn't seem to have a subject. Usually, these are **imperative sentences**, sentences that make a request or command. Imperative sentences always have an implied subject, and that subject is *you*:

Please make your bed before leaving for school.

If you ask *who?* or *what?* is to *make* [your bed before leaving], there isn't a noun or pronoun that will answer that. That is because in imperative sentences, the subject is implied; the answer to the question is always *you*.

What if the sentence is a question? In order to find the subject of a question, simply turn the question into a statement, which will place the subject at the beginning of the sentence:

Why didn't he make his bed before leaving for school?

Restated, it becomes:

S   V   V
He did not make his bed before leaving for school.

Who did not make [his bed]? *He* is the subject.

SIMPLE PREDICATES

A **simple predicate** (or verb) describes the action or condition of the subject or subjects in a sentence. In order to identify the predicate(s) in a sentence, ask *what word shows what the subject(s) is doing?* Or *what word shows the condition of the subject(s)?*

S   S   V
Nathan and Sara helped their mom and dad with the yard work.

Nathan and Sara *did what? Helped* is the predicate. Just as with subjects, there can be more than one predicate in a sentence. When two predicates share the same subject, this is called a **compound predicate**.

S   V   V
Danielle sketched and painted a lovely picture.

Danielle *did what? Sketched* and *painted* are the predicates.

<pre>
            S   S   V   V
</pre>
    Eleanor and Leslie are best friends and always support each other.

Eleanor and Leslie *what*? They *are* (best friends) and they *support. Are* and *support* are the predicates.

COMPLETE SUBJECTS AND COMPLETE PREDICATES

Identifying any sentence's complete subject and complete predicate is easy as well. Once you find the simple subject and the simple predicate, you should be able to notice a natural division between the telling part of the sentence and the doing or condition part. For example:

<pre>
        S   V
</pre>
    Brielle, an artist, | sold some of her art at the auction.

<pre>
        S   V
</pre>
    The birds | always sing early in the morning.

In the first sentence, the subject, *Brielle,* and the appositive phrase that gives more information about Brielle—*an artist*—form the complete subject of the sentence. Likewise, the complete predicate is made up of the verb that tells what Brielle did, *sold,* and other words that give more information about what she sold and where she sold it—*some of her art at the auction.*

Similarly, in the second sentence, notice that the adverb *always* is part of the complete predicate. Even if you didn't know that adverbs modify verbs, you could see that *always* gives more information about the verb *sing,* not the noun *bird,* so it belongs with the complete predicate.

PRACTICE: SUBJECTS AND PREDICATES

Identify the simple subjects and simple predicates of the following sentences, and then divide the sentence into its complete subject and complete predicate. You can check your answers at the end of the lesson.

1. Have a happy birthday.

2. The mountains are a popular vacation spot.

3. Tad took his dog to the vet yesterday.

4. Holly and Mac cleaned the basement.

5. Do birds sing to warn other birds about their territory?

6. Park your car in the garage when the weather calls for snow.

7. At six o'clock each day, please feed and walk the dog.

8. Salad is a healthy addition to lunch and dinner.

9. Skunks are very accurate when they spray a rival.

10. Justin washed and waxed Dad's car.

11. The garbage truck arrives very early in the morning.

12. Would they prefer chili or sauerkraut with their hotdogs?

13. Sixteen inches of snow fell in the Adirondacks last night.

14. I am afraid of heights.

15. Reading often improves your vocabulary.

16. Cell phones are convenient at home or at the office.

17. Grab my hand and hang on tight!

18. The drenching rainfall yesterday flooded many roads.

19. May I borrow your stapler?

20. Place a coaster underneath your glass, please.

ANSWERS

1. S: (You); P: have

(You) | have a happy birthday.

2. S: mountains; P: are

The mountains | are a popular vacation spot.

3. S: Tad; P: took

Tad | took his dog to the vet yesterday.

4. S: Holly and Mac; P: cleaned

Holly and Mac | cleaned the basement.

5. S: birds; P: do sing

Do birds sing to warn other birds about their territory? becomes the statement:

Birds | do sing to warn other birds about their territory.

6. S: (You); P: park

(You) | park your car in the garage when the weather calls for snow.

7. S: (you); P: feed, walk

At six o'clock each day, (you) | please feed and walk the dog.

8. S: salad; P: is

Salad | is a healthy addition to lunch and dinner.

9. S: skunks; P: are

Skunks | are very accurate when they spray a rival.

10. S: Justin; P: washed, waxed

Justin | washed and waxed Dad's car.

11. S: garbage truck; P: arrives

The garbage truck | arrives very early in the morning.

12. S: they; P: would prefer

Would they prefer chili or sauerkraut with their hotdogs? becomes the statement: They | would prefer chili or sauerkraut with their hotdogs.

13. S: snow; P: fell

Sixteen inches of snow | fell in the Adirondacks last night.

14. S: I; P: am

I | am afraid of heights.

15. S: reading; P: improves

Reading | often improves your vocabulary.

16. S: phones; P: are

Cell phones | are convenient at home or at the office.

17. S: (You); P: grab, hang on

(You) | grab my hand and hang on tight!

18. S: rainfall; P: flooded

The drenching rainfall | yesterday flooded many roads.

19. S: I; P: may borrow

May I borrow your stapler? becomes the statement: I | may borrow your stapler.

20. S: (You); P: place

(You) | place a coaster underneath your glass, please.

direct and indirect objects

A sentence is made up of words, a statement is made in words....
Statements are made, words or sentences are used.

JOHN LANGSHAW AUSTIN (1911–1960)
BRITISH PHILOSOPHER

In this lesson, you will learn how an object is often necessary to complete a basic sentence containing an action verb. Objects also make sentences more meaningful to readers and listeners.

A DIRECT OBJECT is the noun or pronoun that is receiving the action from the action verb in the sentence. Finding direct objects in a sentence is simple: They answer *whom?* or *what?* about the action verb.

    S   V   DO
Scott kicked the ball into the net.   Kicked what? [the] ball.

    S   V   DO
Wanda took Sara to the theater.   Took whom? Sara.

There can also be more than one direct object in a sentence. As with compound subjects and compound predicates, when the direct objects share one or more of the same verbs in the sentence, they are called **compound direct objects**.

    S   V   DO   DO
David planted an apple tree and a lemon tree this weekend.

Who planted? *David* is the subject. Planted *what*? An *apple tree* and a *lemon tree* are the direct objects.

```
        S     V    DO       DO
     Nathan plays tennis and soccer.
```

Who plays? *Nathan* is the subject. Plays *what*? *Tennis* and *soccer* are the direct objects.

As well, sentences that have a direct object may also contain an **indirect object**. An indirect object is directly related to the direct object; it tells who or what is the recipient of the direct object. You cannot have an indirect object in a sentence without having a direct object first. To identify an indirect object in the sentence ask *to or for whom?* or *to or for what?* after the action verb. For example:

```
        S     V    IO      DO
     Steven showed Cory his iguana.
```

Who showed? *Steven* did; thus, he is the subject. Showed *what*? An *iguana*; thus, it is the direct object. Showed (an iguana) *to whom*? *Cory*; thus, he is the indirect object.

```
       S    V      IO         DO
     Kayla baked Schneider a cake for his birthday.
```

Who baked? *Kayla* did; thus, she is the subject. Baked *what*? A *cake*; thus, it is the direct object. Baked (a cake) *for whom*? *Schneider*; thus, he is the indirect object.

....

TIP: Indirect objects are always found between the verb and the direct object. Be careful not to mistakenly identify an object of a preposition (OOP) as a direct object:

```
        S    V     DO        OOP
     Margaret sent a postcard to Donna.
```

Even though *Donna* answers to whom Margaret sent the postcard, in this sentence, Donna is an OOP, *not* an indirect object.

```
        S    V    IO       DO
     Margaret sent Donna a postcard.
```

Here, there is no prepositional phrase, and *Donna* is the indirect object receiving the direct object, the postcard.

....

PRACTICE: DIRECT AND INDIRECT OBJECTS

Identify the direct and any indirect objects in the following sentences. You may check your answers on page 84.

1. Denny brought Tony some apples, bananas, and strawberries from the store.

2. Place the puppy into his pen and come to dinner.

3. Jennifer sent an e-mail to her friend in Missouri.

4. The kids played street hockey all afternoon.

5. Thomas got an invitation to visit UCLA during Spring Break.

6. Gary brought a paper to read while he waited for Ann to finish.

7. Justin Timberlake sang his fans' favorite hits.

8. The king gave his most loyal subjects a generous portion of land.

9. The instructor offered her students a lollipop after class.

10. He tied the nets to the goal posts and lined the fields for this season's games.

11. The plumber sent Mom a bill for fixing the sink.

12. Paul bought us tickets for Sunday's game.

13. Grandma read Michael and Mark a story before bed.

14. Orlando wrote a poem and submitted it to the contest.

15. I need more time to finish my project.

ANSWERS

1. IO = Tony; DO = apples, bananas, strawberries
2. DO = puppy
3. DO = e-mail
4. DO = street hockey
5. DO = invitation
6. DO = paper
7. DO = hits
8. IO = subjects; DO = portion
9. IO = students; DO = lollipop
10. DO = nets, fields
11. IO = Mom; DO = bill
12. IO = us; DO= tickets
13. IO = Michael, Mark; DO = story
14. DO = poem, it
15. DO = time

SECTION 3

building a sentence

THE BASIC COMPONENTS of a sentence are essential, but they can be boring if they're the only elements that have been given to the reader or listener. Variety and embellishment are important, too, if one is to become a good writer or effective speaker.

- **Phrases:** strings of two or more "subject and predicate free" words that add information, detail, and bring cohesiveness to ideas within a sentence.
- **Clauses:** like phrases, they also add details to the sentence, except they need the help of a subject and predicate. Sometimes clauses can be called sentences, themselves!
- **Sentence combining:** want to make your sentences more complex and advanced? Learn how to combine like sentences, add phrases and clauses, and you're on your way.
- **Fragments and run-ons:** they stick out like a sore thumb and can compromise your communication goals. Avoid them and know how to spot them for correction.

phrases

Only in grammar can you be more than perfect.
WILLIAM SAFIRE (1929–   )
AMERICAN JOURNALIST

These indispensable and adaptable groups of words add information and detail, and bring cohesiveness to ideas within a sentence. In this lesson, you will learn how phrases help bring structure to your writing.

A PHRASE IS a string of two or more words that can express a thought or function as a single part of speech, like an adjective or an adverb, in a sentence. They do not contain both a subject and a predicate, so they cannot function as a sentence. For example:

Phrases without a Predicate:

that car   Shannon's umbrella   their pool

Phrases without a Subject:

almost hit a tree   broke into pieces   is heated year round

ADJECTIVE AND ADVERB PHRASES

As you may remember from Lesson 8, a prepositional phrase is a phrase that begins with a preposition and ends with a noun or a pronoun (also called an OOP). Within a sentence, prepositional phrases always act as if they were adjectives or adverbs—we call them **adjective phrases** and **adverb phrases**. When functioning like an adjective, the phrase answers *what kind?* or *which one?* about the noun or pronoun it is modifying.

> Dad's polka-dotted tie looked silly.

Here, *polka-dotted* is an adjective telling *what kind* of tie Dad had.

> Dad's tie with polka-dots looked silly.

Here, *with polka-dots* is a prepositional phrase (adjective phrase) acting like an adjective modifying the noun *tie*.

Likewise, when functioning like an adverb, the phrase answers *where? when? how?* or *to what extent?* about the verb, adjective, or adverb it is modifying.

> We will begin class tomorrow.
> We will begin class on Monday.

Tomorrow is an adverb telling *when* about the verb *begin* in the sentence. *On Monday* is a prepositional phrase (adverb phrase) acting like an adverb modifying the verb *begin*. Let's look at another example.

> The ballerina danced gracefully across the stage.
> The ballerina danced with grace across the stage.

The adverb *gracefully* tells how the ballerina danced. The adverb phrase *with grace* also tells how she danced.

APPOSITIVE PHRASES

An **appositive** is a word that renames, identifies, or gives more detail about a noun or pronoun that it follows in the sentence.

> Their son Raul is going to Princeton in the fall.

The noun *son* is being renamed and further identified by the appositive *Raul* in the sentence.

We can also add other modifiers to the appositive *Raul* and make an appositive phrase:

Their son Raul, the oldest of four, is going to Princeton in the fall.

Appositives can also be compound:

Their son Raul, the oldest of four and an outstanding student, is going to Princeton in the fall.

GERUND AND PARTICIPIAL PHRASES

A **gerund phrase** begins with an *-ing* word, or a gerund. Unlike prepositional phrases, gerund phrases act like a noun in a sentence, so you find them acting like subjects or objects.

Walking across the rickety wooden bridge was scary.

Walking across the rickety wooden bridge answers *what was scary?* Thus, it functions as a noun in the sentence.

Don't confuse a gerund phrase with a participial phrase. Like a gerund, a participle ends with *-ing*, but that is the extent of their likeness. A **participial phrase** functions like an adjective in a sentence, describing a noun or a pronoun; a gerund phrase always acts like a noun.

Walking across the rickety wooden bridge, I stepped on each board with caution.

Walking across the rickety wooden bridge is describing the subject *I* in the sentence. Thus, it functions as an adjective.

PRACTICE: PHRASES

Identify the adjective and adverb phrases in the sentences that follow. You may check your answers at the end of the lesson.

1. Students with ambition are usually successful.

2. The painter climbed up the ladder.

3. Her ring with the emeralds and rubies came from her grandmother.

4. I saw the squirrels scampering along the fence rail in the backyard.

5. They anchored their fishing boat about a mile off shore.

Identify the appositive phrases in the following sentences and the noun or pronoun they are modifying.

6. Her adventure story appeared in *Cricket*, the popular children's magazine.

7. Which Shakespearian tragedy do you like most, *King Lear* or *Hamlet*?

8. Would you please give this note to your teacher, Mr. Christopher?

9. My cousin, a sophomore at the Academy of Allied Health and Science, wants to be a physical therapist.

10. Marcie told a story about the Tasmanian Devil, an urban legend.

Determine whether the **boldfaced** phrase is a gerund phrase or a participial phrase.

11. Trying to be protective, Charlotte put her parakeet back into its cage.

12. Misplacing my belt with the silver buckle disappointed Dad.

13. Snoring with contentment, Hallie's cat slept on the bed by her feet.

14. **Having to wait at the bus stop** for over an hour every day was becoming tiring.

15. **Heading this year for the Super Bowl** is our favorite team, the New York Giants.

ANSWERS

1. adjective phrase: with ambition
2. adverb phrase: up the ladder
3. adjective phrase: with the emeralds and rubies
   adverb phrase: from her grandmother
4. adverb phrase: along the fence rail, in the backyard
5. adverb phrase: about a mile off shore
6. the popular children's magazine; modifies: *Cricket*
7. *King Lear* or *Hamlet*; modifies: tragedy
8. Mr. Christopher; modifies: teacher
9. a sophomore at the Academy of Allied Health and Science; modifies: cousin
10. an urban legend; modifies: Tasmanian Devil
11. participial phrase
12. gerund phrase
13. participial phrase
14. gerund phrase
15. participial phrase

clauses

*At painful times, when composition is impossible and
reading is not enough, grammars and dictionaries
are excellent for distraction.*
ELIZABETH BARRETT BROWNING (1806–1861)
ENGLISH POET

Sometimes they're a sentence, and sometimes they're not. Clauses, like phrases,
add detail and information to your sentences. In this lesson, you will see how
and why clauses are necessary elements within a piece of work.

UNLIKE A PHRASE, a **clause** is a group of words that has its own subject and
verb. This allows some clauses to be considered sentences. Others, despite the
fact that they have their own subject and verb, are not sentences because they
don't express a complete thought. There are three kinds of clauses: independent,
subordinate, and relative. Let's look at them more closely.

INDEPENDENT CLAUSES

The **independent clause**, or **main clause**, can stand alone as a simple sentence,
because it not only has the two main components of a sentence, a simple subject and a simple predicate, but it also expresses a complete thought.

      S   V   S   V
Henry walked home from school.   It began to rain.

Two or more clauses can be put together, with the help of semicolons or coordinating conjunctions (*and, or, for, nor, but, yet,* and *so*), to form a longer sentence.

> Henry walked home from school; it began to rain.
>
> Henry walked home from school *and* it began to rain.
>
> Henry walked home from school *and* it began to rain, *but* luckily he had an umbrella stashed in his book bag; he is always prepared.

We will learn more about combining clauses to make longer sentences in Lesson 14.

SUBORDINATE CLAUSES

A **subordinate clause**, also referred to as a **dependent clause**, cannot stand alone as a simple sentence, even though it contains a subject and a verb. Such clauses must be connected with an independent clause to help them do their job.

> S   V   V   S   V
> Although Cara was absent from school for three days, she did well on her quiz.
>   [subordinate]   +   [independent]

> S   V   S   V
> Dean's mom cooked dinner while he worked on his science project.
>   [independent]   +   [subordinate]

Even though they may look similar to independent clauses, subordinate clauses are different because they must begin with either a **subordinating conjunction** or a **relative pronoun**. The following charts give some examples.

COMMON SUBORDINATING CONJUNCTIONS

after	although	as if	as long as	as much as
as soon as	because	before	even if	even though
if	in order that	now that	provided that	since
so	so long as	though	unless	until
when	whenever	whereas	whether	while
where				

Examples:	*after* she left *so long as* I am the leader *whether* you like it or not

RELATIVE PRONOUNS

that	which	whichever
who	whoever	whose
whosever	whom	whomever

Examples: *whose* mom is so nice *which* made him grouchy *whichever* comes first

TIP: When you begin a sentence with a subordinate clause, you have to put a comma after it.

Whether I like it or not, Mom says I must wear my helmet when I skateboard.

However, when you end a sentence with one, you don't.

Mom says I must wear my helmet when I skateboard whether I like it or not.

RELATIVE CLAUSES

A **relative clause** is one that begins with a relative pronoun (see the preceding chart). In a sentence, a relative clause acts like an adjective by giving more information about the subject of the sentence. Even though relative clauses have their own subject and verb, though, they cannot stand alone as a sentence because they don't express a complete thought. For example:

Mom's apple pie recipe that won in last week's county fair was published in the local newspaper.

that won in last week's county fair answers *which one?* about the noun *recipe*.

Austin, who skis well, will compete for a state title this year.

who skis well answers *which one?* about the proper noun *Austin*.

PRACTICE: INDEPENDENT AND SUBORDINATE CLAUSES

Determine whether the boldfaced group of words is an independent, a subordinate, or a relative clause. You may check your answers with the key at the end of the lesson.

1. **Jason took a nap** before he left for his friend's house.

2. You can keep your privileges **as long as we continue to see progress**.

3. Hannah wasn't feeling well, **which Dad noticed immediately**.

4. **Although you may disagree**, I still say Sheila is the best person for the job.

5. There would be less tension between them **if they could just see eye to eye**.

6. **I'm bringing my homework along** even though we don't plan to stay long.

7. Golam, **whom I've never met before**, seemed like a pretty nice guy.

8. **In order that we may be respectful of the presenters**, please turn off your cell phones.

9. I knew this was going to be an exciting game **when Andrew took his first swing**.

10. Margaret, **whose earrings I borrowed last week**, told her dad that she was tired and wanted to go home.

11. **Before you go**, would you please be sure to clean up the mess you make?

12. **It seemed like only yesterday** that I was here playing tag with my friends Julie and Laurie.

13. **Whichever cookie you decide on**, I assure you it will be absolutely delicious.

14. Since she was only just around the corner, **Paula decided to walk to the store instead of driving**.

15. **Whoever she is**, she sure seems to know what she's doing.

ANSWERS

1. independent
2. subordinate
3. relative
4. subordinate
5. subordinate
6. independent
7. relative
8. subordinate
9. subordinate
10. relative
11. subordinate
12. independent
13. relative
14. independent
15. relative

combining sentences

*Grammar is the logic of speech, even as logic
is the grammar of reason.*
RICHARD C. TRENCH (1807–1886)
ENGLISH ARCHBISHOP AND POET

If you want your sentences to be more complex and advanced, you must know how to combine sentences. Learn how to do just that in this lesson.

DO YOU REMEMBER when you were first learning to read? Most of the sentences you practiced with were simple and short, which was very helpful. Now that you're an advanced reader, you would find those same sentences monotonous and uninteresting. Good readers like sentences that vary in length and complexity; writers achieve this through sentence combining.

SIMPLE SENTENCES

We know that simple sentences (independent clauses) contain a simple subject and a simple predicate. Look at the following combinations you could use to make a basic simple sentence (these examples don't include any words, phrases, or clauses that could be added for detail).

SIMPLE SENTENCE STRUCTURES

(Implied subject *you*) + (V)erb = simple sentence
Listen!

(S)ubject + V = simple sentence
Sara plays.

S + V + (O)bject = simple sentence
Sara plays piano.

(C)ompound S + V + O = simple sentence
Sara and Katelyn play piano.

S + CV + O = simple sentence
Sara dances and plays piano.

S + V + CO = simple sentence
Sara plays piano and tennis.

CS + CV + O = simple sentence
Sara and Katelyn dance and play tennis.

CS + V + CO = simple sentence
Sara and Katelyn play piano and tennis.

S + CV + CO = simple sentence
Sara dances and plays piano and tennis.

CS + CV + CO = simple sentence
Sara and Katelyn dance and play piano and tennis.

NOTE: While only two names or items are given in the compound examples, three or more could be included. Also note that all the subjects and objects share the same verbs.

Now, let's look at two other basic sentence types in writing: the **compound sentence** and the **complex sentence**.

COMPOUND SENTENCES

When we combine two independent clauses (or simple sentences) into one sentence, we create a **compound sentence**. Creating compound sentences helps make our writing less choppy. To do this, we take two or more topic-related sentences and join them together with one of the coordinating conjunctions (*for, and, nor, but, or, yet,* or *so*) or join them with a semicolon.

The sun was shining. The weather was warm. I went to the beach.

Some possible combinations would be:

> The sun was shining *and* the weather was warm, *so* I went to the beach.
>
> The weather was warm *and* the sun was shining, *so* I went to the beach.
>
> I went to the beach *for* the sun was shining *and* the weather was warm.
>
> The sun was shining *and* the weather was warm; I went to the beach.
>
> The weather was warm *and* the sun was shining; I went to the beach.
>
> I went to the beach: The sun was shining *and* the weather was warm.

The coordinating conjunction *or* works well in sentences where choice is involved, and *nor* works well when the expressions are negative. Using *but* and *yet* works well in sentences where there is dissimilarity between the expressions.

PRACTICE 1: COMPOUND SENTENCES

Combine the following simple sentences to create a compound sentence. You can check your answers beginning on page 103.

1. It rained for three days. The streets in my neighborhood flooded.

2. I got to ball practice late. I forgot to set my alarm.

3. Kyle completed his homework. He put it in his binder.

4. Luke mowed the lawn. He earned ten dollars.

5. I stayed up late last night. I am tired today.

6. Neil doesn't like seafood. He doesn't like cabbage.

7. My pencil was broken. I borrowed one from Jake.

8. I like apples. I like pears more.

9. Eight people got into the elevator. It was crowded. Three people got off.

10. Georgia gathered the pictures. She could arrange them in a special album for her family.

COMPLEX AND COMPOUND-COMPLEX SENTENCES

Complex sentences follow the same idea as compound sentences, except that they are made up of one independent clause and one or more subordinate (dependent) clauses. For example:

> Because the weather was warm, I went to the beach.
>
> I went to the beach because the weather was warm.

Let's add another subordinate clause:

> I went to the beach because the weather was warm, even though it was a weekday.
>
> Because the weather was warm, I went to the beach, even though it was a weekday.
>
> Even though it was a weekday, because the weather was warm, I went to the beach.
>
> I went to the beach even though it was a weekday, because the weather was warm.

Finally, there are **compound-complex sentences**, which have at least two independent clauses and one or more subordinate clauses:

> Even though it was a weekday and I should have been in school, I went to the beach.
>
> I went to the beach even though it was a weekday and I should have been in school.

Let's add another subordinate clause:

> Because the weather was warm, I went to the beach, even though it was a weekday and I should have been in school.

PRACTICE 2: COMPLEX AND COMPOUND-COMPLEX SENTENCES

Identify the independent and subordinate clauses in the following sentences and determine whether they are complex or compound-complex. You can check your answers on page 104.

11. Jason decided to stay up late because he had a lot of homework to do.

12. If you hurry, we might get to school on time.

13. Although Monica had a cold, she went to school because she had a test.

14. While washing the car, Todd slipped on the soap and he fell.

15. Dad takes the train to work even though he has a car.

16. After Mom arrived, she put the disk in the DVD player and we watched a great movie.

17. Even though his heart pounded with dread, Ben bolted up the stairs, and he checked out the strange noise.

18. Molly baked brownies since she had nothing else to do.

19. Karen made a list of what was needed, and she double-checked it so she wouldn't forget anything.

20. Frank had a good sense of humor, so he laughed a lot.

ANSWERS

Practice 1: Compound Sentences

(In each case, only one possible answer is shown.)

1. It rained for three days, so the streets in my neighborhood flooded.
2. I got to ball practice late for I forgot to set my alarm.
3. Kyle completed his homework and he put it in his binder.
4. Luke mowed the lawn and he earned ten dollars.
5. I stayed up late last night so I am tired today.
6. Neil doesn't like seafood, nor does he like cabbage.
7. My pencil was broken so I borrowed one from Jake.
8. I like apples, but I like pears more.

9. Eight people got into the elevator, but it was crowded, so three people got off.

10. Georgia gathered the pictures so she could arrange them in a special album for her family.

Practice 2: Complex and Compound-Complex Sentences

(The independent clauses are **boldfaced**, the subordinate clauses are *italic*, and conjunctions are Roman.)

11. **Jason decided to stay up late** *because he had a lot of homework to do.* (complex)

12. *If you hurry,* **we might get to school on time**. (complex)

13. *Although Monica had a cold,* **she went to school** *because she had a test.* (complex)

14. *While washing the car,* **Todd slipped on the soap** and **he fell**. (compound-complex)

15. **Dad takes the train to work** *even though he has a car.* (complex)

16. *After Mom arrived,* **she put the disk in the DVD player** and **we watched a great movie**. (compound-complex)

17. *Even though his heart pounded with dread,* **Ben bolted up the stairs**, and **he checked out the strange noise**. (compound-complex)

18. **Molly baked brownies** *since she had nothing else to do.* (complex)

19. **Karen made a list of what was needed**, and **she double-checked it** *so she wouldn't forget anything.* (compound-complex)

20. **Frank had a good sense of humor**, so *he laughed a lot.* (complex)

fragments and run-ons

If you make yourself understood, you're always speaking well.
MOLIERE (1622–1673)
FRENCH PLAYWRIGHT

Knowing whether or not you have a sentence fragment or run-on in your writing is essential. Learn how to avoid making these mistakes and how to identify them if you make them.

FRAGMENTS

A **fragment** is an incomplete sentence. Sometimes it lacks a subject or a verb.

No verb: Without a care in the world.

No subject: Took the dog to the vet for a check up.

Other times it is just a dependent clause (a clause that has a subject and a verb, but begins with a subordinating conjunction). Incomplete sentences like these can often be fixed just by eliminating the end punctuation and combining them with the adjoining sentence, adding any necessary proper punctuation.

Incorrect: Our high school has many sports teams. Such as soccer, tennis, lacrosse, baseball, and football.

Correct: Our high school has many sports teams, such as soccer, tennis, lacrosse, baseball, and football.

....

TIP: A newspaper is one place where fragments run rampant. This is because of the costly space restrictions and the abundance of advertising. If you look, you'll find sentence fragments in headlines, captions, titles, and ads. They tend to be short and snappy—easy to remember.

Note: Writing in fragments, like in a newspaper, does not reflect formal writing etiquette and should not be used in writing for business or school. Save this journalistic style for news reporting only.

....

RUN-ONS

Run-on sentences can sneak up on you when you least expect it this usually occurs when you are writing quickly and not putting punctuation where it's needed.

This sentence is one kind of run-on, called a **fused sentence**. You get a fused sentence when you combine two or more complete sentences without any punctuation mark. There are actually two separate sentences in the example above. Do you see them? We can solve our fused sentence issue in one of three different ways. Let's see how.

One way is to insert a period after each complete sentence (and, of course, capitalizing the first word of your new sentences).

Run-on sentences can sneak up on you when you least expect it. This usually occurs when you are writing quickly and not putting punctuation where it's needed.

If the sentences in your run-on are topic related, then you can also insert a semicolon between them.

Run-on sentences can sneak up on you when you least expect it; this usually occurs when you are writing quickly and not putting punctuation where it's needed.

Lastly, you can place a comma and a coordinating conjunction (*for, and, nor, but, or, yet,* or *so*) into the sentence.

Run-on sentences can sneak up on you when you least expect it, **for** this usually occurs when you are writing quickly and not putting punctuation where it's needed.

Another common type of run-on sentence, called a **comma splice**, occurs when you use a comma instead of the appropriate end punctuation.

Run-on sentences can sneak up on you when you least expect it, this usually occurs when you are writing quickly and not putting punctuation where it's needed.

To solve this mistake, you need to add an appropriate coordinating conjunction (*for, and, nor, but, or, yet,* or *so*).

Run-on sentences can sneak up on you when you least expect it, **for** this usually occurs when you are writing quickly and not putting punctuation where it's needed.

The wayward comma can also be replaced with another punctuation mark, such as a semicolon or a period.

Run-on sentences can sneak up on you when you least expect it; this usually occurs when you are writing quickly and not putting punctuation where it's needed.

Run-on sentences can sneak up on you when you least expect it. This usually occurs when you are writing quickly and not putting punctuation where it's needed.

One last way to fix these mistakes is to reword the sentences into a complex sentence (one independent clause with one subordinate clause).

When you are writing quickly and not putting punctuation where it's needed, run-on sentences can sneak up on you when you least expect it.

PRACTICE: FRAGMENTS AND RUN-ONS

Determine whether the following word groups are complete sentences (C), fragments (F), or run-ons (R). Revise any run-on. You can check your answers at the end of the chapter.

1. Thought that the Shakespeare play was confusing.

2. Mix the ground beef with the chopped onion and pepper then add the bread crumbs and egg.

3. While they raked the leaves.

4. No one could make heads or tails of the very unusual sculpture.

5. We made plans to get together at Charlotte's house later on during the week we had a lot of catching up to do.

6. Because it's supposed to rain.

7. If Lillian gets here late, she'll be eliminated from the competition.

8. Our town recycles cans, bottles, and newspapers.

9. I don't know.

10. When Julie went to Paris she visited the Louvre Museum, the Eiffel Tower she also visited the Champs-Elysées.

ANSWERS

1. F
2. R—Mix the ground beef with the chopped onion and pepper. Then add the bread crumbs and egg.
3. F
4. C
5. R—We made plans to get together at Charlotte's house later on during the week. We had a lot of catching up to do.
6. F
7. C
8. C
9. C
10. R—When Julie went to Paris, she visited the Louvre Museum and the Eiffel Tower. She also visited the Champs-Elysées.

SECTION 4

agreement

Like the run-on sentence or sentence fragment, poor subject–verb agreement and antecedent–pronoun agreement can tarnish the messages you're communicating to listeners and readers. Recognizing these mistakes is the first step to correcting them, and ultimately steering clear of them altogether.

- **Subject–verb agreement:** singular subjects belong with single verbs, and plural subjects belong with plural verbs—verbs and subjects must be compatible in number and person.
- **Pronoun–antecedent agreement:** pronouns help us avoid having to repeat the same noun over and over again; however, knowing *what* or *whom* the noun is referring to in the first place is also essential. Balance is the key. Agreement in *gender*, *number*, and *person* is vital for clarity.

subject–verb agreement

Language is fossil poetry.
RALPH WALDO EMERSON (1803–1882)
AMERICAN POET

Along with fragments and run-ons, poor subject–verb agreement will detract from your writing and distort your meaning. In this lesson, learn how to steer clear of this writing faux pas.

IT IS ESSENTIAL that all of the subjects and verbs in your writing (and speaking) are compatible in both number and person. If your sentence has a singular subject (referring to only one person, place, or thing), then it must be coupled with a singular verb. Likewise, if your sentence has a plural subject (referring to more than one person, place, or thing), then it must be coupled with a plural verb.

Singular: Tommy plans to run in the cross-country race.

The dog likes to sleep on the porch under the rocking chair.

Plural: Kevin and Nathan usually shoot hoops on Saturdays.

The bees fly from flower to flower gathering pollen.

Most verbs are easily recognizable in our writing and speaking—they tend to move the sentence along—so when any subject–verb agreement is incorrect, it is so easily recognizable. This is especially true of the verb *be*, the most widely used verb form in the English language. The table below shows it is conjugated according to number, form, and person.

CONJUGATION OF THE VERB *BE*

Person	Subject	Present Tense	Past Tense
First/Singular	I	am	was
First/Plural	we	are	were
Second/Singular	you	are	were
Second/Plural	you	are	were
Third/Singular	he, she, it	is	was
Third/Plural	they	are	were

Even though we may hear the verb *be* used casually (and quite widely in some instances) in spoken language, this usage is incorrect in standard English. *Be* only follows a subject in a sentence when it's coupled with a helping verb (for example, *can be, should be, will be, could be*).

Incorrect:	She be going to school late this morning.
	We be going late, too.
Correct:	She is going to school late this morning.
	We are going late, too.

COMPOUND SUBJECTS AND VERBS

Sometimes you may have two or more subjects sharing the same verb; this is referred to as a **compound subject**. When you have a compound subject, you must use the conjunctions *and*, *or*, or *neither . . . nor* to connect them together.

Mom *or* Dad was supposed to pick us up at the movies.

Neither Mom *nor* Dad was supposed to pick us up at the movies.

Mom *and* Dad are supposed to pick us up at the movies.

TIP: When you use the conjunctions *or* or *nor*, the subjects are thought of as separate units, and therefore take a singular verb. The same is true for plural subjects joined by *or* or *nor*, except that the verb used will be plural.

Note that when the conjunction *and* is used, the verb is plural. That is because with *and*, the subjects are looked at as equals, and become compound. So, the verb must be plural. NOTE: There are some exceptions to this. Some compound subjects are looked upon as a single unit. For example: *spaghetti and meatballs*, *macaroni and cheese*, and *peanut butter and jelly*.

What do you do if you have a sentence that contains a singular and a plural subject? Deciding whether to use a singular or plural verb may seem tricky, but the solution is quite simple. Whichever subject is mentioned last in the sentence, whether singular or plural, determines the correct verb to use:

Is it the cats or the *dog* that *is* making such a commotion?

Is it the dog or the *cats* that *are* making such a commotion?

INDEFINITE PRONOUNS

Words such as *anybody*, *someone*, *most*, and *none* are very general when referring to people, places, or things. They are called **indefinite pronouns**. With only a handful of exceptions, it is pretty simple to tell whether most indefinite pronouns are singular or plural.

INDEFINITE PRONOUNS

	Singular		Plural	Both
anybody	everything	one	both	all
anyone	little	other	few	any
anything	much	somebody	many	more
each	neither	someone	others	most
either	nobody	something	several	none
everybody	no one			some
everyone	nothing			

Like any other pronoun, a singular indefinite pronoun takes a singular verb, and a plural one takes a plural verb. Some indefinite pronouns can be both, so the noun that the indefinite pronoun refers to determines the appropriate verb.

Most of the *glasses are* broken.

Most of the *glass is* broken.

PRACTICE: SUBJECT–VERB AGREEMENT

Identify the verb that correctly agrees with the subject in each sentence. You may check your answers with the key at end of the lesson.

1. Most of this soccer equipment (belong, belongs) to the township.

2. The delivery of milk (arrive, arrives) each morning at six o'clock.

3. Peanut butter and jelly (is, are) my favorite lunch.

4. The students (walk, walks) quickly to get to class on time.

5. Several pieces of lawn furniture (need, needs) to be replaced.

6. Drama Club (meet, meets) on Tuesdays and Thursdays at three o'clock.

7. Mr. and Mrs. Jones (commute, commutes) to the city by train.

8. The big oak tree in the front yard (shade, shades) our front porch most of the day.

9. Sue or Jill (is, are) likely to be voted this year's prom queen.

10. Nothing ever (seem, seems) to bother him.

ANSWERS

1. Most of this soccer equipment *belongs* to the township.
2. The delivery of milk *arrives* each morning at six o'clock.
3. Peanut butter and jelly *is* my favorite lunch.
4. The students *walk* quickly to get to class on time.
5. Several pieces of lawn furniture *need* to be replaced.
6. Drama Club *meets* on Tuesdays and Thursdays at three o'clock.
7. Mr. and Mrs. Jones *commute* to the city by train.
8. The big oak tree in the front yard *shades* our front porch most of the day.
9. Sue or Jill *is* likely to be voted for this year's prom queen.
10. Nothing ever *seems* to bother him.

pronoun–antecedent agreement

I never made a mistake in grammar but one in my life and as soon as I done it I seen it.

CARL SANDBURG (1878–1967)
AMERICAN POET

Ante-what? *And how do I make sure it's compatible with my pronoun?* In this lesson, you will learn how to make your pronouns and antecedents exist in harmony with one another.

PRONOUNS ALLOW US to refer repeatedly to a specific noun without saying the word over and over again.

Without: Lucas thought Lucas saw a ghost, but Lucas wasn't sure.

With: Lucas thought he saw a ghost, but he wasn't sure.

As you learned in Lesson 2, a **pronoun** is a word that takes the place of a noun (see the following chart of common pronouns for review). The **antecedent** is the word that the pronoun has replaced in the sentence.

Mom made Jack take a nap. He was grumpy.

The pronoun in this sentence refers to the antecedent, *Jack*. Since Jack is one boy, the third-person singular pronoun *he* was used instead of *she* or *they*. That is so there is agreement in gender, number, and person between the antecedent and its pronoun. This kind of agreement is very important. Imagine if it didn't matter. We could have sentences that sound like gibberish.

> Gina folded towels. He was helping Mom with the laundry. We planned to do homework afterward because I had a test tomorrow in chemistry.

It is obvious that *Gina* is a female, so the only appropriate pronoun would be *she*, not *he*, *we*, or *I*.

It is important that the pronoun–antecedent agreement be clear to avoid confusion.

> Holly and Betsy went to the park to play Frisbee and have a picnic with their friends Greg and Josh. They were having a great time until she accidentally tripped over his foot and they bumped heads, giving her a headache.

Whose foot? Did Holly trip over Greg's foot or Josh's? Or was it Betsy who tripped? Who bumped heads? Holly and Betsy? Holly and Greg? Holly and Josh? Betsy and Greg? Betsy and Josh? Lastly, who got the headache? Holly or Betsy? Get the point?

....

TIP: Sometimes pronouns can make a sentence so confusing that it might be best not to use any pronouns at all.

> **Confusing:** Lori, Sue, and Renee are finally going to the mall to go dress shopping for the prom. She had made plans to go last week, but they called and canceled at the last minute.
>
> **Better:** Lori, Sue, and Renee are finally going to the mall to go dress shopping for the prom. Sue had made plans to go last week, but Lori and Renee called and canceled at the last minute.

....

COMMON PRONOUNS

all	another	any	anybody	anyone
anything	both	each	either	everybody
everyone	everything	few	hers	herself
himself	his	I	its	itself
many	me	mine	myself	neither
no one	nobody	none	nothing	one
others	ours	ourselves	she	some
somebody	someone	something	that	theirs
them	themselves	these	they	this
us	we	what	which	who
whom	whose	you	yours	yourself
yourselves				

Some of the pronouns in the preceding chart are obviously singular or plural. Others, though, might not be as apparent, such as the indefinite pronouns *anyone, anybody, either, neither, everybody, everyone, everything, no one, nobody, somebody, someone, each, none,* and *one.* All of these pronouns are considered singular in number and are compatible only with singular pronouns.

Incorrect: Everyone placed their books on the table.

Correct: Everyone placed his or her books on the table.

Incorrect: Each student did their homework.

Correct: Each student did his or her homework.

The indefinite pronouns *all, more, none, most, any,* and *some,* when used before a prepositional phrase, can be seen as either singular or plural, depending upon the OOP (object of the preposition) at the end of the phrase. Use that noun to help you decide which pronoun would be compatible.

Plural: Most of the peaches were ripe. They smelled delicious.

Singular: Most of the floor was mopped. It looked sparkling clean.

PRACTICE: PRONOUN–ANTECEDENT AGREEMENT

Determine which pronoun best fits for pronoun–antecedent agreement in each sentence. Check your answers on the following page.

1. Somebody dropped (their/his or her) wallet.

2. Most of the class pushed in (their/its) chairs.

3. Some of the girls sang (their/her) favorite song.

4. Katelyn and Radikha called (their/her) parents on Saturday.

5. Daniel or Dave left (their/his) sunglasses on the table in the hallway.

6. Neither Mary nor Paul studied (their/his or her) spelling words.

7. All of the players liked (their/his or her) coach.

8. Everybody must wash (their/his or her) hands before dinner.

9. Many good athletes spend (their/his or her) time training after school.

10. One of the buildings lost (their/its) electricity yesterday afternoon.

11. These puppies still belong with (their/his or her) mother.

12. Nobody broke (their/his or her) promise.

13. Nora placed (their/her) watch on the shelf by her bed.

14. Rick or Davaughn brought (their/his) guitar.

15. Most dogs are loyal to (their/his or her) owner.

ANSWERS

1. his or her
2. their
3. their
4. their
5. his
6. his or her
7. their
8. his or her
9. their
10. its
11. their
12. his or her
13. her
14. his
15. their

S E C T I O N 5

punctuation

PUNCTUATION MARKS LEAD the reader through sentences much like road signs lead a driver along the road. Proper placement of the numerous punctuation marks used in the English language is necessary, and not doing so can drastically alter the meaning of your sentence.

- **Endmarks:** periods, question marks, and exclamation points indicate to the reader that the sentence is complete and that he or she should briefly pause before moving on to the next sentence.
- **Commas:** commas perform many functions. They indicate pause by the reader and set items apart from one another for different reasons within sentences, letters, and numbers.
- **Colons and semicolons:** these are two of the trickiest punctuation marks. They can introduce and emphasize items, or connect and separate items.
- **Quotation marks:** these are found mainly in dialogue; they also distinguish someone's exact words for the reader.
- **Underlining and italicizing:** they are typically interchangeable in use—for emphasis and separation.
- **Brackets and parentheses:** these allow writers to provide extra information to clarify the contents of their sentences.
- **Hyphens and dashes:** these are helpful in dividing, joining, interrupting, and emphasizing writers' words and phrases.

- **Apostrophes:** apostrophes help make a writer's words show possession and contract.
- **Capitalization:** we capitalize more than just the first word of a sentence—titles, words in dialogue, proper nouns, and proper adjectives should also be capitalized.

endmarks

No iron can pierce the heart with such force
as a period put just at the right place.
ISAAC BABEL (1894–1940)
RUSSIAN JOURNALIST

Knowing how and where to end your sentences is the key to helping your reader understand your writing. In this lesson, you will learn the proper placement and meanings of these basic punctuation marks.

PUNCTUATION IS ESSENTIAL in writing. The various internal and external punctuation marks we use are like road signs for readers. Our **endmarks**—periods, question marks, and exclamation points—indicate that the thought or sentence is complete and that the reader should pause, much in the way a stop sign signals a driver.

PERIODS

The **period** is the most common form of end punctuation. It indicates the end of a declarative sentence—a statement, a request, or a command.

I am cold.
Please close the window.

We also find periods in common abbreviations, like those for months, days, and measurements.

inches = in.   square feet = sq. ft.   Monday = Mon.   September = Sept.

We also find periods in a person's initials

Franklin D. Roosevelt   E. B. White   J. F. Kennedy

and in name titles.

Mister = Mr.   Doctor = Dr.   President = Pres.

....

TIP: If an abbreviation ending in a period is the last word in a sentence, the abbreviation's period will also act as the endmark (in other words, the sentence will not end with two periods).

> **Incorrect:**   The next bus leaves at 8:30 A.M..
>
> **Correct:**   The next bus leaves at 8:30 A.M.

The exception to this is if the sentence ends with an exclamation point or a question mark:

> Does the next bus leave at 8:30 A.M.?
>
> The next bus leaves at 8:30 A.M.!

....

QUESTION MARKS

We find **question marks** at the end of interrogative sentences, also known as questions.

> Can Trish play tennis?   Are you hungry?   What time is it, please?

Be careful not to confuse an **indirect question** with a direct question. Since indirect questions are really just statements (declarative sentences), they take a period, not a question mark.

Direct:	Why did Lionel wear a green sock on one foot and a purple one on the other?
Indirect:	Dale wondered why Lionel wore a green sock on one foot and a purple one on the other.

EXCLAMATION POINTS

When you want to imply strong feeling or emotion in a written sentence, you should place an **exclamation point** at the end. This would also include authoritative commands and interjections.

Hey! Watch what you're doing!

Thanks! I love it!

....

TIP: Many people use two or more exclamation points at the end of words or sentences they want to stress.

Oh my gosh!!!! I don't know what I was thinking!!! I'm SO sorry!!!!!!

If one shows emphasis, two or three must really show emphasis, right? In a note to a friend, that's okay. But in formal writing, it's best to use just one.

....

PRACTICE: ENDMARKS

Determine whether each of these sentences is properly punctuated. Then check your answers using the key at the end of the lesson.

1. It's 2 A.M.! You should be asleep!

2. How nice that Joseph offered to help clean up afterward?

3. What is the capital of Missouri?

4. I asked Carl to meet me at 3 P.M. to study.

5. Put your glasses away in a safe place.

6. Sh!!!! Be careful not to wake the baby?

7. We are supposed to head home at around 9:00 P.M..

8. Nonsense! I would never say that?

9. In yesterday's track meet, did Luke's high jump measure over 6 ft.?

10. How sad June must feel?

Add the correct punctuation in each sentence. Then check your answers using the key at the end of the lesson.

11. Mrs Tomaino lives across the street

12. Excellent job, Kayla I knew you could do it if you put your mind to it

13. Rev Bill Turner spoke at a youth conference in St Louis this past weekend

14. The itinerary shows that the tour starts at 8 AM and goes to 4:30 PM

15. Colfax Jct is the third stop before reaching Highland Borough

16. Gee why did Mark leave late He promised to be here by 10 AM

17. Peter was 4 ft 7 in tall in Jan It's Nov now, and he's almost 5 ft 1 in

18. Dr Lorimer said Paul should exercise for one hr on Mon, Wed, and Fri

19. Ouch That hurt my toe

20. I was wondering if Ashley saw Haley yesterday in school

ANSWERS

1. correct

2. incorrect

Answer: How nice that Joseph offered to help clean up afterward.

3. correct

4. correct

5. correct

6. incorrect

Answer: Sh! Be careful not to wake the baby.

Sh! Be careful not to wake the baby!

7. incorrect

Answer: We are supposed to head home at around 9:00 P.M.

8. incorrect

Answer: Nonsense! I would never say that.

Nonsense! I would never say that!

9. correct

10. incorrect

Answer: How sad June must feel.

11. Mrs. Tomaino lives across the street.

12. Excellent job, Kayla! I knew you could do it if you put your mind to it.

13. Rev. Bill Turner spoke at a youth conference in St. Louis this past weekend.

14. The itinerary shows that the tour starts at 8 A.M. and goes to 4:30 P.M.

15. Colfax Jct. is the third stop before reaching Highland Borough.

16. Gee! Why did Mark leave late? He promised to be here by 10 A.M.

17. Peter was 4 ft. 7 in. tall in Jan. It's Nov. now, and he's almost 5 ft. 1 in.

18. Dr. Lorimer said Paul should exercise for one hr. on Mon., Wed., and Fri.

19. Ouch! That hurt my toe!

20. I was wondering if Ashley saw Haley yesterday in school.

commas, part 1

The writer who neglects punctuation, or mispunctuates,
is liable to be misunderstood for the want of merely a comma,
it often occurs that an axiom appears a paradox,
or that a sarcasm is converted into a sermonoid.
EDGAR ALLAN POE (1809–1849)
AMERICAN POET

In this lesson, we will look at how commas are used in sentences. Knowing where and when commas are appropriate is essential.

COMMAS WITHIN A SENTENCE

A **comma** is an internal punctuation mark (endmarks are external) that tell the reader when to pause. By setting apart some words, phrases, and clauses, commas add clarity to the sentence. There are several basic rules for comma placement. If you follow them, you will not risk having too many or too few commas, either of which could leave your readers confused.

RULE 1: Use commas to separate words, phrases, or clauses in a series.

Red, green, and blue are the only colors left to choose from.

Jamie untied the bow, opened the box, and peeked inside.

If your series uses the words *and* or *or* to connect them, then commas are not necessary.

Red or green or blue are the only colors left to choose from.

Jamie untied the bow and opened the box and peeked inside.

RULE 2: Use commas to separate two or more adjectives that are describing a noun or pronoun in the same way. If you can put *and* between them, or reverse them, and the sentence remains logical, a comma belongs between the words.

    Incorrect: The *little, old* lady sat with her cat on the porch.

    Test 1:   The *little and old* lady sat with her cat on the porch.

    Test 2:   The *old, little* lady sat with her cat on the porch.

    Correct: Put the *short, stubby* bushes on the side of the tall ones.

    Test 1:   Put the *short and stubby* bushes on the side of the tall ones.

    Test 2:   Put the *stubby, short* bushes on the side of the tall ones.

RULE 3: Use a comma to set off an introductory word or phrase from the rest of the sentence.

Without a comma, your reader could mistakenly carry the meaning of the introduction into the main part of the sentence.

    Confusing: While they ate the students talked about their plans for the weekend.

    Less Confusing: While they ate, the students talked about their plans for the weekend.

RULE 4: Use commas to set off an appositive, a word or phrase that renames or identifies the noun or pronoun preceding it.

Our neighbors, the Dixons, traveled to Yellowstone National Park for vacation this summer.

RULE 5: Use a comma before a coordinating conjunction (*for, and, nor, but, or, yet,* or *so*) that is followed by an independent clause.

Fried chicken is delicious, *but* it is also fattening.

RULE 6: Use commas when writing dialogue.

For a direct quotation that identifies the speaker first, place the comma outside the opening quotation marks, after the opening phrase.

Vera replied, "It is nice to meet you, too."

For a direct quotation with an interrupter, place one comma after the first portion of the quoted sentence and another comma after the interrupter words.

"I think," Vera continued, "that we have met before."

Note that commas are not used when an indirect quotation states what someone said, but not exactly in the same words (see Lesson 22).

Vera said that she thought they had met before.

PRACTICE: COMMAS WITHIN A SENTENCE

Add commas where necessary in the following items. You can check your answers on the following page.

1. Marie's fat Siamese cat lounged in the front window.

2. The large scary bug crawled quickly across the bedroom floor.

3. We ate chips salsa pretzels pizza and popcorn during the movie.

4. "How many days" Juan continued "do we have off of school?"

5. The elephant in the center ring had leathery skin a long trunk and big floppy ears.

6. "I really hope David makes it to practice" said Frankie.

7. Mark Twain an American writer was famous worldwide.

8. Well what is your opinion about this?

9. Besides skateboarding and surfing John also plays baseball and soccer.

ANSWERS

1. Marie's fat Siamese cat lounged in the front window. (No comma is needed: neither "Marie's Siamese fat cat . . ." nor "Marie's Siamese *and* fat cat . . ." makes sense.)
2. The large, scary bug crawled quickly across the bedroom floor.
3. We ate chips, salsa, pretzels, pizza, and popcorn during the movie.
4. "How many days," Juan continued, "do we have off of school?"
5. The elephant in the center ring had leathery skin, a long trunk, and big floppy ears.
6. "I really hope David makes it to practice," said Frankie.
7. Mark Twain, an American writer, was famous worldwide.
8. Well, what is your opinion about this?
9. Besides skateboarding and surfing, John also plays baseball and soccer.

commas, part 2

My attitude toward punctuation is that it ought to be as conventional as possible. The game of golf would lose a good deal if croquet mallets and billiard cues were allowed on the putting green . . .

ERNEST HEMINGWAY (1899–1961)
AMERICAN NOVELIST

Commas are also used when writing the date, addressing a formal letter, and in separating components of a large number. In this lesson, you'll learn how to use commas in these various formats.

COMMAS WITH LETTERS AND NUMBERS

The list of comma rules continues to show you how commas are used in correspondence, with dates, with professional titles, and within large numbers.

RULE 7: Use commas between the day of the month and the year when you are writing the date.

When dates are written, commas are placed after the day

September 22, 1964   January 1, 2008   May 4, 1945

and after the day of the week if it is noted.

Saturday, February 2, 1985   Tuesday, June 18, 2002

Note: Dates that are written numerically do not contain commas, and instead use slashes.

3/17/93   5/21/91   12/26/57

....

TIP: No comma is necessary if only the month and the day, or the month and the year, are written.

Neil and Nelly arrive on August 12.

Neil and Nelly arrive in August 2008.

....

RULE 8: Use commas when properly addressing an envelope and heading a letter.

Letter/Envelope Format: Mr. and Mrs. W. J. Milling
59 Pecan Drive
Selma, AL 36701

When addressing an envelope or letter, place a comma only between the city and state of the address. Notice that there is no comma between the state and the zip code.

Sentence Format: Please send the following order of yellow roses to Mr. and Mrs. W. J. Milling, 59 Pecan Drive, Selma, AL 36701.

When writing an address within a sentence, commas are placed between the person's name and street address, between the street address and the city, and between the city and state.

TIP: When writing the name of a city and state within a sentence, you _must_ place a comma after the name of the state before continuing the sentence:

> We often travel to Orlando, Florida, in the fall because the weather is cooler.

The same rule applies when you mention a city and country name:

> Chiang Mai, Thailand, is a beautiful place to visit as well.

When you write a friendly letter, use a comma after the person's name in the greeting. (In business letters, use a colon instead.) All letters require a comma after the closing.

> 1257 Perkins Avenue
> Succasunna, NJ 07876
> July 31, 2008

Dear Rose,

Thank you so much for inviting Neil and Nelly to spend a week with you in the Pocono's. They should be arriving on Tuesday, August 12, around noon. We will arrive on Wednesday the 20th to pick them up. They are looking forward to the trip!

> Sincerely,
> Susan and Bob

Note: Friendly letters are the only letter where you place a comma after the salutation. In a business letter, a colon (:) is used instead. Both letters require a comma after the closing, however.

	Friendly Letters	**Business Letters**
Opening	Dear Mema, Dear Betsy,	To Whom It May Concern: Dear Sir:
Closing	Love, Yours truly, Fondly,	Sincerely, Sincerest regards, Best regards,

RULE 9: Use commas to set off titles and degrees after a person's name.

Dolores Burwell, M.D.   Mark Di Sanctis, Ph.D.

However, if you are addressing the person as doctor, omit the comma:

Dr. Storlazi   Dr. Kevin Rich

RULE 10: Use commas when writing numbers longer than three digits.
Long numbers can be difficult to read without commas. The rule for placing commas in long numbers is simple: Put a comma after every group of three numbers, counted from right to left. This helps identify the groups by their value place (hundreds, thousands, millions, and so on).

5319874621348 = 5, 319, 874, 621, 348 = 5,319,874,621,348

(5-trillion, 319-billion, 874-million, 621-thousand, 3-hundred and 48)

....

TIP: There are several exceptions to this comma rule:

Phone numbers	201-282-4337
Zip codes	35701
Years	1985
Serial numbers	7H927C378945
House numbers	18904 Wexler Street

However, when numbers are written in a series, commas should be placed between the items:

Mary's children were born in 1989, 1991, 1995, and 1999.

....

PRACTICE: COMMAS WITH LETTERS AND NUMBERS

Insert commas where necessary in these sentences, phrases, and numbers. Check your answers on the following page.

1. Jill bought the house at 5824 Mt. Holly Oak Drive Jonestown MD.

2. Sara's fifteenth birthday is March 17 2009.

3. Dear Martha

4. 42398762015200

5. Anita Marcus DMD is one of the dentists speaking at our meeting today.

6. Truly yours

7. 46738692975432698643225982

8. The Space Shuttle had successful missions in 2000 2001 2002 2003 2005 2006 2007 and 2008.

9. Dear Mr. Hughes Mr. Foley Mr. Drake and Mr. Lynch:

10. Mike's new address is 128 Girard Avenue Roxbury WV 87654.

ANSWERS

1. Jill bought the house at 5824 Mt. Holly Oak Drive, Jonestown, MD.

2. Sara's fifteenth birthday is March 17, 2009.

3. Dear Martha,

4. 42,398,762,015,200

5. Anita Marcus, DMD, is one of the dentists speaking at our meeting today.

6. Truly yours,

7. 4,673,869,297,543,269,864,325,982

8. The Space Shuttle had successful missions in 2000, 2001, 2002, 2003, 2005, 2006, 2007, and 2008.

9. Dear Mr. Hughes, Mr. Foley, Mr. Drake, and Mr. Lynch:

10. Mike's new address is 128 Girard Avenue, Roxbury, WV 87654.

colons and semicolons

Sometimes you get a glimpse of a semicolon coming, a few lines farther on, and it is like climbing a steep path through woods and seeing a wooden bench just at a bend in the road ahead, a place where you can expect to sit for a moment, catching your breath.

LEWIS THOMAS (1913–1993)
ENGLISH SCIENTIST

Next to commas, colons and semicolons are two of the trickiest punctuation marks. In this lesson, you will find out where these types of punctuation belong and why.

COLONS

The **colon** is used to introduce a list, statement, or phrase within a sentence; it gives emphasis to the items that follow it.

List: To make a basic salad, include the following items: lettuce, carrots, tomato, cucumber, and onion.

Statement: The rule was clear: Absolutely no food or drinks are allowed.

Phrase: There was one thing I forgot to write down on my test: my name!

TIP: Not all lists require a colon. Do not use a colon after a preposition or a verb:

Incorrect:	Please bring two pencils, graphing paper, and a calculator to: room 201, room 202, or room 203.
	The brownies are: delicious, chocolaty, and rich.
Correct:	Please bring two pencils, graphing paper, and a calculator to room 201, room 202, or room 203.
	The brownies are delicious, chocolaty, and rich.

Colons are also used to introduce a lengthy quotation

According to President Abraham Lincoln: "You can fool some of the people all of the time, and all of the people some of the time, but you cannot fool all of the people all of the time."

and to introduce the subtitle of a movie or book.

Book:	*Wolf Rider: A Tale of Terror* is an exciting mystery adventure novel written by Avi.
Movie:	Stanley Kubrick's film *2001: A Space Odyssey* is almost completely silent.

Colons separate the minutes from the hour in written time

The train headed for Cincinnati departs from the station at 6:47 A.M.

and separate the volume and issue number, and the volume and page numbers, of books and magazines.

Scientific American 9:20 [volume 9, issue 20]

National Geographic 48:14–19 [volume 48, pages 14–19]

Use a colon to end the salutation of a business letter.

Dear Mr. Dunlap:

To Whom It May Concern:

Dear Sir/Madam:

SEMICOLONS

The **semicolon** is used to connect two independent clauses whose topics are related.

> Our house is a dingy gray color; it needs painting badly.

> My uncle owns a car wash; we get free car washes during the summer.

The house's dingy gray color and the fact that it needs painting are closely related. The semicolon helps emphasize this.

Semicolons are also used to connect two independent clauses that are separated by a conjunctive adverb (see the following chart).

> Our house was a dingy gray color; hence, it got painted.

> My uncle owns a car wash; consequently, we get free car washes during the summer.

COMMON CONJUNCTIVE ADVERBS

afterward	accordingly	besides
certainly	consequently	furthermore
hence	however	indeed
instead	in fact	in addition
likewise	moreover	naturally
nevertheless	nonetheless	otherwise
similarly	so	still
then	therefore	thus

Additionally, semicolons separate items in a series that already contain commas themselves.

> The planning committee for the prom included Cheryl, the class president; Carol, the vice president; Julie, the treasurer; Mark, the committee chairman; Kevin, a co-chairman; and Mr. Michaels, the senior class advisor.

PRACTICE: COLONS AND SEMICOLONS

Add colons and semicolons where necessary in these sentences. You may check your answers on the following page.

1. Scott used his sister's cell phone to call Kris he lost his yesterday.

2. Liz will meet Kim and Erin at [six o'clock] they have a yoga class at [fifteen minutes after six o'clock].

3. We watched *Garfield A Tail of Two Kittens* after school on Monday.

4. [*TIME* volume number 4, pages 56–75.]

5. Add these to your list when you go to the grocery store bread, milk, lunch meat, and cheese.

6. Shari owns four dogs three of them are poodles.

7. Helen Keller once said "The best and most beautiful things in the world cannot be seen or even touched. They must be felt within the heart."

8. Dear Dr. Klinger

9. Lexi likes knitting scarves and hats Gina likes watercolor painting and Mona likes making pottery.

10. Our plane leaves at [four o'clock] in the morning therefore, we will leave at [one o'clock] to be sure we arrive on time.

11. *Harry Spy Aficionado of Fourth Street* tops Orland's list of favorite books.

12. Kayla's school supply list included a calculator, ruler, and protractor for math a composition book, pocket dictionary, and pens for English and a binder.

13. [*Newsweek*, volume number 5, issue number 26, pages 22–29.]

14. Ursula will go on stage at [five minutes after six o'clock] Mallory will follow shortly after at [eight minutes after six o'clock] and we'll wrap it up with Sue at [twenty minutes after six o'clock].

15. Dear Congressman Henderson

ANSWERS

1. Scott used his sister's cell phone to call Kris; he lost his yesterday.
2. Liz will meet Kim and Erin at 6:00; they have a yoga class at 6:15.
3. We watched *Garfield: A Tail of Two Kittens* after school on Monday.
4. *TIME* 4:56–75
5. Add these to your list when you go to the grocery store: bread, milk, lunch meat, and cheese.
6. Shari owns four dogs; three of them are poodles.
7. Helen Keller once said: "The best and most beautiful things in the world cannot be seen or even touched. They must be felt within the heart."
8. Dear Dr. Klinger:
9. Lexi likes knitting scarves and hats, Gina likes watercolor painting, and Mona likes making pottery.
10. Our plane leaves at 4:00 in the morning; therefore, we will leave at 1:00 to be sure we arrive on time.
11. *Harry: Spy Aficionado of Fourth Street* tops Orland's list of favorite books.
12. Kayla's school supply list included a calculator, ruler, and protractor for math; a composition book, pocket dictionary, and pens for English; and a binder.
13. *Newsweek* 5: 26: 22-29
14. Ursula will go on stage at 6:05; Mallory will follow shortly after at 6:08; and we'll wrap it up with Sue at 6:20.
15. Dear Congressman Henderson:

quotation marks

I often quote myself. It adds spice to my conversation.
GEORGE BERNARD SHAW (1856–1950)
IRISH PLAYWRIGHT

Dialogue can move stories along and bring a character to life more than plain words can. Knowing how to punctuate different forms of dialogue correctly is useful for all writers, and this lesson will show you how to do just that.

QUOTATION MARKS ARE used in writing to signify the exact words that someone has said, which we call a **direct quotation**. Direct quotations require the use of opening and ending quotation marks.

"If your homework is finished, you may go to the movies with Charles," Mom told Peter.

. . . .

TIP: When someone merely refers to what someone else said rather than repeating it exactly, that is called an **indirect quotation**. Do not use quotation marks with indirect quotations

Mom told Peter that he could go to the movies with Charles if his homework was finished.

or for someone's thoughts:

Incorrect: "Mom is being reasonable," thought Peter.

Correct: Mom is being reasonable, thought Peter.

. . . .

When writing a quotation, you must capitalize the first word.

Fred whined, *"Gee*, I'm hungry."

The only exception is when the quotation has an interrupter. Unless the continuation begins with a proper noun, a proper adjective, or the pronoun *I*, the first word of the continuation begins with a lowercase letter.

"I thought," continued Fred, *"we* were going to eat lunch an hour ago."

Notice that each part of the quotation is enclosed in quotation marks. Also note that the first part of the quote ends with a comma (indicating that more will follow) and the interrupting words are followed by a comma before the quotation continues.

Only periods, question marks, and exclamation points are placed inside the end quotes of a quotation. Colons and semicolons should be placed on the outside.

Notice that a comma is placed before the opening quotes when they are preceded by introductory words (such as *said*, *stated*, or *interjected*).

Hannah said, "This concert is great!"; her friends agreed.

TIP: Sometimes, question marks and exclamation points belong outside the quotation marks. This occurs when the entire sentence calls for that punctuation mark. For example:

Why did Lindsay say "Michael will not go"?

You annoy me when you say "I can't"!

When a quote is a statement that ends with a period, but concluding words follow the quotation, you must change the period to a comma.

"I don't like spinach or asparagus," Raul said.

Quotation marks can be used—but only sparingly—to indicate sarcasm or irony.

Anxious to meet her friends, Shelby quickly "cleaned" her room so she could leave.

This sentence implies that Shelby did not clean her room in the manner expected. She cleaned her room quickly and with little effort.

PRACTICE: QUOTATION MARKS

Properly insert quotation marks, commas, and endmarks into these sentences. You may check your answers using the key at the end of the lesson.

1. Wow Those are terrific pictures exclaimed James

2. My sister would like to go to the movies with us said Gina May she

3. This summer promises continued Roger to be a very memorable one for sure

4. Would you care for another slice of pizza asked Mom

5. Why did you say I'm better than she is

6. Mrs. Miller said she wanted the tree projects on her desk first period tomorrow

7. Mrs. Gardner added We should find out tomorrow

8. The car sighed Dad needs to be taken to the mechanic

9. Nick said that he wasn't feeling well yesterday

10. We have to finish this quickly or we'll get in trouble cried Katie

11. Which one of you said I can't swim

12. Why does Karla say I think I know but I'm not sure

13. Here is the hammer you asked for said Richard

14. Perhaps you wouldn't be so tired suggested Dad if you went to bed earlier

15. Excellent work Paul praised Mom

ANSWERS

1. "Wow! Those are terrific pictures!" exclaimed James.
2. "My sister would like to go to the movies with us," said Gina. "May she?"
3. "This summer promises," continued Roger, "to be a very memorable one for sure."
4. "Would you care for another slice of pizza?" asked Mom.
5. Why did you say, "I'm better than she is"?
6. Mrs. Miller said she wanted the tree projects on her desk first period tomorrow.
7. Mrs. Gardner added, "We should find out tomorrow."
8. "The car," sighed Dad, "needs to be taken to the mechanic."
9. Nick said that he wasn't feeling well yesterday.
10. "We have to finish this quickly or we'll get in trouble!" cried Katie.
11. Which one of you said, "I can't swim"?
12. Why does Karla say, "I think I know but I'm not sure"?
13. "Here is the hammer you asked for," said Richard.
14. "Perhaps you wouldn't be so tired," suggested Dad, "if you went to bed earlier."
15. "Excellent work, Paul!" praised Mom.

italicizing and underlining

Grammar is a piano I play by ear.
All I know about grammar is its power.
JOAN DIDION (1934–   )
AMERICAN AUTHOR

Italics and underlines are useful forms of punctuation for emphasis and setting certain groups of words apart from others. In this lesson, you will learn why and how these features help your writing.

ITALICIZING AND UNDERLINING are interchangeable in use. Before typewriters and computers, writing was done by hand, so italicizing words was difficult, if not impossible. Therefore, underlining was used to emphasize words. Technology now allows us to use one or the other as we please.

Grammar and usage dictates when we should use italics and underlining and when we shouldn't. Here are key areas you will find them in writing.

RULE 1: Italicize or underline the titles of long written works, such as books, magazines, movies, TV shows, newspapers, plays, musicals, and albums or CDs.

Gary Paulsen's novel *Hatchet*   Gary Paulsen's novel <u>Hatchet</u>

The New York Times   <u>The New York Times</u>

Shakespeare's play *Romeo and Juliet*   Shakespeare's play <u>Romeo and Juliet</u>

the Broadway hit *A Chorus Line*   the Broadway hit <u>A Chorus Line</u>

....

TIP: Be consistent! Don't *italicize* one title and <u>underline</u> the next one. Pick one style and then stick to it.

....

Exception: Do not underline or italicize the titles of holy books, such as the Bible, the Tanakh, or the Koran. The names of chapters or books within these works are also not underlined or italicized: I Corinthians, Genesis, Yusuf.

....

TIP: Use quotation marks around the titles of stories, songs, short poems, articles, and other smaller-sized works.

> Aesop's fable "The Boy Who Cried Wolf" (short story)
>
> Francis Scott Key's "The Star Spangled Banner" (song)
>
> Shel Silverstein's "Sick" (short poem)
>
> "Making Recycling Really Pay" (article)

....

RULE 2: Italicize or underline foreign words.

> *Madame* Kondoleon greeted the class by saying *bonjour!*
>
> <u>Madame</u> Kondoleon greeted the class by saying <u>bonjour</u>!
>
> *Senora* Reyes shared the *platano* with her class.
>
> <u>Senora</u> Reyes shared the <u>platano</u> with her class.

Note, however, that many foreign words have become part of the English language, and need not be italicized; for example, hacienda, kibitz, and taco. (When in doubt, check your dictionary.)

RULE 3: Italicize or underline words you want to emphasize.

When we speak, our tone of voice can emphasize words and imply meaning. When we write, we can use italics or underlines to do the same thing.
    Can you tell the difference in the meanings of these four sentences?

> Jane was overjoyed.   [Okay, Jane was overjoyed.]
>
> *Jane* was overjoyed.   [It wasn't anyone; it was *Jane* who was overjoyed.]

Jane *was* overjoyed.   [Jane's no longer overjoyed.]

Jane was *overjoyed*.   [Jane wasn't just happy, she was *overjoyed*.]

RULE 4: Italicize onomatopoeia (sound words).

Brrrr! It's freezing out here. Let's get inside where it's warm.

Clink! Clank! Carefully trying to make it from the dining room to the kitchen with the stack of dishes, Olivia tripped on the bump in the rug and the mountain of dirty dishes fell—*crash!*—to the floor.

PRACTICE: ITALICIZING AND UNDERLINING

Identify words or phrases that need underlining or italicizing in the following sentences. You may check your answers with the key at the end of the lesson.

1. "Au revoir mes étudiants," my French professor said to his students.

2. The bee went bzzz as it flew past my ear.

3. The shelf to your left has the Chicago Times, the New York Times, USA Today, and the L.A. Times; the one on the right has the news magazines TIME, Newsweek, and U.S. News and World Report.

4. Number the Stars, written by Lowis Lowry, is an engaging novel set in Denmark.

5. How do you know it's what she wants?

6. The flyer says that in Act I of the play Wicked the chorus sings "No One Mourns the Wicked."

7. The Book of Revelations is in both the Holy Bible and the Jewish Tanakh.

8. The box kite took to the wind and ZOOM flew over the trees and disappeared into the sky.

9. I heard the sizzle of the steak on the grill as Dad barbequed. Mmmm, I couldn't wait until dinner. Buon appetito!

10. Use the clues in brackets to italicize / underline the appropriate word in each sentence.
I was shocked by the look she gave me. [Her look was more than I bargained for]
I was shocked by the look she gave me. [I'm no longer shocked]
I was shocked by the look she gave me. [No one else was shocked but me]
I was shocked by the look she gave me. [How dare she give that look to me]
I was shocked by the look she gave me. [It wasn't what she said that shocked me]

ANSWERS

1. *"Au revoir mes étudiants,"* my French professor said to his students.

2. The bee went *bzzz* as it flew past my ear.

3. The shelf to your left has *The Chicago Times*, *The New York Times*, *USA Today*, and the *L.A. Times*; the one on the right has the news magazines *TIME*, *Newsweek*, and *U.S. News and World Report*.
or
The shelf to your left has the <u>Chicago Times</u>, <u>The New York Times</u>, <u>USA Today</u>, and the <u>L.A. Times</u>; the one on the right has the news magazines <u>TIME</u>, <u>Newsweek</u>, and <u>U.S. News and World Report</u>.

4. *Number the Stars*, written by Lowis Lowry, is an engaging novel set in Denmark.
or
<u>Number the Stars</u>, written by Lowis Lowry, is an engaging novel set in Denmark.

5. How do *you* know it's what she wants?
How do you know it's what *she* wants?

6. The flyer says that in Act I of the play *Wicked* the chorus sings "No One Mourns the Wicked."
or
The flyer says that in Act I of the play <u>Wicked</u> the chorus sings "No One Mourns the Wicked."

7. The Book of Revelations is in both the Holy Bible and the Jewish Tanakh.

8. The box kite took to the wind and *ZOOM* flew over the trees and disappeared into the sky.

9. I heard the sizzle of the steak on the grill as Dad barbequed. *Mmmm,* I couldn't wait until dinner. *Buon appetito!*

10. I was *shocked* by the look she gave me. [Her look was more than I bargained for]

I *was* shocked by the look she gave me. [I'm no longer shocked]

I was shocked by the look she gave me. [No one else was shocked but me]

I was shocked by the look she gave *me*. [How dare she give that look to me]

I was shocked by the *look* she gave me. [It wasn't what she said that shocked me]

parentheses and brackets

Grammar is the logic of speech, even as logic
is the grammar of reason.
RICHARD C. TRENCH (1807–1886)
ENGLISH ARCHBISHOP AND POET

Sometimes adding comments or afterthoughts to your own writing or to someone else's (called editorializing) is necessary to enhance meaning. In this lesson, you will learn how to do this correctly.

PARENTHESES ALLOW WRITERS to provide extra information (in the middle or at the end) to clarify the contents of their sentences. When information is placed inside parentheses, it is called a **parenthetical comment**. Of the two punctuation marks you'll learn about in this lesson (brackets and parentheses), parentheses are more prevalent—not only because they have more uses in ordinary writing, but also because they are more functional in areas besides writing (have a look at your math book, for example).

RULE 1: Place information inside parentheses when you want to provide your reader with extra information (in the middle, or even at the end, of your sentence).

We ice skated (or should I say fell-skated) most of the morning at the pond behind the old barn.

....

TIP: Parenthetical comments are disposable; the sentence would still make sense without them.

....

RULE 2: Numbers (such as dates, page numbers, itemizing numbers, and the like) are frequently placed inside parentheses.

George Washington (1732–1799) was born in Westmoreland County, Virginia.

More information regarding the childhood of President Washington can be found in Chapter 2 (pp. 14–23).

Make sure you do the following before you hand in your essay: (1) revise for sentence flow, (2) edit for grammar and spelling mistakes, and (3) place the proper heading on the title page.

or

Make sure you do the following before you hand in your essay: (a) revise for sentence flow, (b) edit for grammar and spelling mistakes, and (c) place the proper heading on the title page.

RULE 3: Use parentheses for numerals that repeat and confirm a written number. This is sometimes done for clarity, and it is an optional rule to parenthetical usage.

Enclosed, please find thirty (30) sharpened pencils and fifteen (15) calculators for testing this week.

RULE 4: Use parentheses to enclose abbreviations or acronyms for spelled-out titles and names (or vise versa).

The American Civil Liberties Union (ACLU) helps protect the rights of all citizens.

The UNICEF (United Nations Children's Fund) home office is located on the UN Plaza, in New York City.

RULE 5: Enclose an alternative form of a written term in parentheses.

Read the page(s) attached and respond ASAP.

[*Interpretation:* Read the page (or pages if there is more than one) attached.]

Please include the name(s) of family member(s) accompanying you.

[*Interpretation:* Please include the name (or names) of family member (or family members, if there is more than one).]

BRACKETS

Brackets help writers clarify information by allowing them to insert an explanation or directions for the reader.

RULE 6: When you want to editorialize or insert your own comments within quoted material, use brackets rather than parentheses.

"[The legendary rock n' roller] Elvis Presley is loved by nearly everyone worldwide," stated Elvis's Fan Club President K. P. Jenkins.

[In this example, the words in the brackets "The legendary rock n' roller" were added to the original quotation "Elvis Presley is loved by nearly . . ." by the author of the written sentence.]

RULE 7: When altering the capitalization of a word within a quote to make it fit into your sentence or paragraph scheme, use brackets.

Follow your teachers to the auditorium in a quiet and orderly fashion.

Altered: Mrs. Vasta's directions to the students were clear: "[f]ollow your teachers to the auditorium in a quiet and orderly fashion."

"The captain mans the ship's helm each morning while his crew has breakfast."

Altered: The crew member reported, "The captain [manned] the ship's helm each morning while his crew [had] breakfast."

PRACTICE: PARENTHESES AND BRACKETS

Insert parentheses and brackets as appropriate in these sentences. You may check your answers using the key at the end of the lesson.

1. The tour guide noted that we may a have lunch at a local restaurant, b at the restaurant on the ship, or c at the cafe by the pool.

2. We built we tried at least a small oval wall out of fieldstones for the flower garden.

3. The National Education Association NEA boasts nearly three million members.

4. Paramecia use their cilia to gather microorganisms like bacteria and algae see pg. 147.

5. It was an exciting weekend what a reunion!

6. The AAA American Automobile Association, serving America since 1921, has millions of loyal members.

7. Pocahontas c.1595–1617 was the daughter of a Powhatan chief.

8. "It the Trojan horse was one of the most cleverly plotted red herrings decoys created by the Greeks," stated Mr. Clark, our world history teacher.

9. Be sure to perform the experiment steps in the following order: 1 carefully take one section of a peeled onion in your hand, 2 with a pair of tweezers gently secure and peel a piece of membrane, 3 place the membrane on a microscope slide, 4 place one drop of iodine on the membrane, and 5 place the slide under the microscope to observe the cell walls of the membrane.

10. "Molly Aunt May's first cousin Jody's second daughter traveled all the way from Seattle to attend the wedding," explained Lila.

ANSWERS

1. The tour guide noted that we may (a) have lunch at a local restaurant, (b) at the restaurant on the ship, or (c) at the cafe by the pool.
2. We built (we tried at least) a small oval wall out of fieldstones for the flower garden.
3. The National Education Association (NEA) boasts nearly three million members.
4. Paramecia use their cilia to gather microorganisms like bacteria and algae (see pg. 147).
5. It was an exciting weekend (what a reunion)!
6. The AAA (American Automobile Association), serving America since 1921, has millions of loyal members.
7. Pocahontas (c.1595–1617) was the daughter of a Powhatan chief.
8. "It [the Trojan horse] was one of the most cleverly plotted red herrings [decoys] created by the Greeks," stated Mr. Clark, our world history teacher.
9. Be sure to perform the experiment steps in the following order: (1) carefully take one section of a peeled onion in your hand, (2) with a pair of tweezers gently secure and peel a piece of membrane, (3) place the membrane on a microscope slide, (4) place one drop of iodine on the membrane, and (5) place the slide under the microscope to observe the cell walls of the membrane.
10. "Molly [Aunt May's first cousin Jody's second daughter] traveled all the way from Seattle to attend the wedding," explained Lila.

hyphens and dashes

Language exerts hidden power, like the moon on the tides.

RITA MAE BROWN (1944—   )
AMERICAN WRITER

In this lesson, you will learn how hyphens and dashes help you divide, join, interrupt, and emphasize your words and phrases. These small but powerful punctuation marks can make a bold impact on the messages you are conveying to your audience.

THOUGH THEY MAY look very similar, **hyphens** and **dashes** do two completely different things in writing. Depending on their usage in a sentence, hyphens can either divide or join, and dashes can either interrupt or emphasize. Learning the difference is easy, as is using them correctly in your writing. Let's see how.

HYPHENS

You can use hyphens in many ways: to divide a word at the end of a line, to join numbers and some compound words, and to attach prefixes to others words.

When used to divide a word at the end of a line of writing, the hyphen is placed in a very specific spot—at any of the syllable breaks in the word or between any double consonants of a word. (Note that one-syllable words, like *brick*, *swim*, or *knife*, cannot be divided or hyphenated.)

sim-pli-fy   re-spon-si-bil-i-ty   ap-pear-ance

All words have one or more **syllables**—individual spoken units. To find the number of syllable breaks in a word, you can tap your finger on the table or your lap, or clap your hand, for each spoken unit of the word. For example, take the word *bird*. When you say *bird*, you can tap or clap for only one syllable. Now let's try the word *refrigerator*. Tap as you say each syllable: *re* (tap) *frig* (tap) *er* (tap) *a* (tap) *tor* (tap). This word has five syllables: *re-frig-er-a-tor*. You can hyphenate the word at any of the four syllable breaks.

re-frigerator   refrig-erator   refriger-ator   refrigera-tor

Hyphens are also used to link prefixes such as *great-*, *ex-*, and *self-*, and the suffix *-elect*, to base words, to create new words such as *great-grandfather*, *ex-boyfriend*, *self-directed*, and *president-elect*.

Hyphens are also used in compound words like *jack-in-the-box* and *father-in-law*; spelled-out numbers from twenty-one through ninety-nine, in fractions (*one-fourth, one-ten-thousandth*), in scores, (*the Yankees won 7-3*), and in dates (*12-31-2008*).

Lastly, hyphens are especially helpful in combining words whose spelling would make the new word appear awkward. For instance, if you wanted to say that something, say buttons, looked like shells, you might say that they were *shell-like*. Without the hyphen, the word would have three *l*s in a row: *shelllike*, which would be very awkward.

DASHES

Dashes can emphasize a word or a phrase, or they can identify the word or phrase as an afterthought.

George's painting is—I don't know—weird.

A dash can also be used like a colon, to set off a short series of words or phrases within a sentence.

Look at what's left—some chips, a half-eaten roll, and a soggy pickle.

PRACTICE: HYPHENS AND DASHES

Hyphenate these words in the appropriate places, if necessary. You may check your answers using the key at the end of the lesson.

1. baggage

2. track

3. happy

4. mother in law

5. friendly

6. please

7. giggle

8. rusty

9. balloon

10. alphabet

Write out the numbers listed below, using hyphens when necessary.

11. 435

12. $\frac{9}{12}$

13. 2,944

14. 11

15. $\frac{1}{2}$

Add hyphens and dashes where needed in these sentences.

16. My greatgrandfather Dad's granddad lived to be ninety eight years old.

17. "I will have to ask my sisters in law what their plans are for Christmas," said Joan.

18. Laura decided to major in prelaw when she was a sophomore at Yale.

19. This warmup jacket is actually too warm.

20. This hightech alarm clock a present from my mom is too complicated to use.

ANSWERS

1. bag-gage
2. track (none needed)
3. hap-py
4. mother-in-law
5. friend-ly
6. please (none needed)
7. gig-gle
8. rus-ty
9. bal-loon
10. alpha-bet
11. four hundred thirty-five
12. nine-twelfths
13. two thousand nine hundred forty-four
14. eleven
15. one-half
16. My great-grandfather—Dad's granddad—lived to be ninety-eight years old.
17. "I will have to ask my sisters-in-law what their plans are for Christmas," said Joan.
18. Laura decided to major in pre-law when she was a sophomore at Yale.
19. This warm-up jacket is actually too warm.
20. This high-tech alarm clock—a present from my mom—is too complicated to use.

apostrophes

If the English language made any sense, a catastrophe
would be an apostrophe with fur.

DOUG LARSON (1902–1981)
ENGLISH GOLD MEDALIST AT PARIS OLYMPICS, 1924

The apostrophe is also part of the small but powerful group of punctuation marks. In this lesson, you will see how they make your words contract and show possession.

WE USE THE apostrophe to create contractions, like *don't* and *couldn't*, and to make nouns possessive, like *Harry's* goldfish and the *rabbit's* cage.

CONTRACTIONS

The word *contract* (pronounced with the stress on the second syllable—*con-TRACT*) means to press together or shorten. When you squeeze two words together to make another word, that's called a **contraction**. For instance, the words *can* and *not* can be written as the contraction *can't*. Many contractions are used in speech and in informal writing (formal writing etiquette discourages the use of slang and contractions).

CONTRACTIONS OF COMMON PRONOUNS

		am/are ↓	will ↓	have/has ↓	had/would ↓
I	→	I'm	I'll	I've	I'd
you	→	you're	you'll	you've	you'd
he	→	he's	he'll	he's	he'd
she	→	she's	she'll	she's	she'd
it	→	it's	it'll	it's	it'd
they	→	they're	they'll	they've	they'd
we	→	we're	we'll	we've	we'd

CONTRACTIONS OF HELPING VERBS

is	+	not	→	isn't
are	+	not	→	aren't
was	+	not	→	wasn't
were	+	not	→	weren't
have	+	not	→	haven't
has	+	not	→	hasn't
had	+	not	→	hadn't
might	+	not	→	mightn't
can	+	not	→	can't
do	+	not	→	doesn't, don't
did	+	not	→	didn't
should	+	not	→	shouldn't
would	+	not	→	wouldn't
could	+	not	→	couldn't

POSSESSIVE NOUNS

A **possessive noun** implies ownership of something by that person, place, or thing (the noun). To make a singular noun—like *boy*, *dog*, or *school*—possessive, add -'s.

> the boy's yo-yo   the school's bleachers   the kite's tail

Be careful not to confuse the plural form of a noun for its possessive form.

Plural Form:	His parents drove us to school.
Singular Possessive:	We went to school in his parent's car.

The first sentence indicates that two parents drove to school. The second sentence indicates that the car of only one parent was driven to school.

To form the possessive of a plural noun (for example, *parents*) simply add an apostrophe after the final *s*.

Plural Possessive:	We went to school in his parents' car.

This sentence implies that the car belongs to both of his parents, not just one.

This rule applies to all plural nouns ending with an *s*. Irregular plural nouns not ending in *s* (*children, women, mice*) follow the rule for singular possessives:

children's   women's   mice's

....

TIP: There are only a very few words whose plural is formed with an apostrophe: numbers, letters, abbreviations, and expressions like *umm, uh,* and *hmm.* For example:

  Ph.D., M.D.   →   Ph.D.'s , M.D.'s

I have two friends who are M.D.'s and three who have Ph.D.'s.

  A, B, C,   →   A's, B's, C's,

She received two A's and three B's on her report card this marking period.

  1, 2, 3,   →   1's, 2's, 3's,

Please try to write your 4's and 9's more clearly; they look too much alike.

  umm, uh, hmm   →   umm's, uh's, hmm's

Try to avoid umm's and uh's when you are giving a speech.

....

TIP: Only one possessive—*its*—does not require an apostrophe. If you mistakenly add an apostrophe to *it* to make it possessive, you are actually forming the contraction meaning *it is*, usually creating utter nonsense:

The puppy wagged it's tail. → The puppy wagged it is tail.

PRACTICE: APOSTROPHES

Place apostrophes where they belong in the following sentences. You may check your answers on the opposite page.

1. I havent heard from Daniel in a week.

2. Lindas best friends name is Grace.

3. It wasnt Tricias fault that Kyles keys got lost.

4. Our schools policy on tardiness is strict.

5. One of her blouses buttons is missing.

6. The books title sounded corny, but its exciting plot kept me reading all night.

7. Why arent we going to Jodis party this afternoon?

8. The salesclerks bright smile was all I needed to lift my spirits.

9. Be sure to check that the bikes tires are inflated properly.

10. The weathermans prediction of a blizzard made everyone anxious.

ANSWERS

1. I haven't heard from Daniel in a week.
2. Linda's best friend's name is Grace.
3. It wasn't Tricia's fault that Kyle's keys got lost.
4. Our school's policy on tardiness is strict.
5. One of her blouse's buttons is missing.
6. The book's title sounded corny, but its exciting plot kept me reading all night.
7. Why aren't we going to Jodi's party this afternoon?
8. The salesclerk's bright smile was all I needed to lift my spirits.
9. Be sure to check that the bike's tires are inflated properly.
10. The weatherman's prediction of a blizzard made everyone anxious.

L E S S O N 27

capitalization

The words of the world want to make sentences.
GASTON BACHELARD (1884–1962)
FRENCH PHILOSOPHER

In addition to words that are capitalized at the beginning of sentences, we capitalize other words for very specific reasons. In this lesson, you will learn when and why these "other words" are capitalized.

AS YOU HAVE already learned, the first word of a sentence is always capitalized. This provides a visual clue for the reader that a new sentence is beginning, especially when several sentences are grouped together, as in a paragraph.

The first word of a direct quotation (a person's exact spoken words) is also capitalized:

"Really, I'm so tired I could sleep standing up," moaned Frank.

The only time we don't capitalize the first word of a direct quotation is when the quotation is continued after an interrupter (such as *she said* or *he replied*):

"I told you," Frank's mom scolded, "not to stay up so late last night!"

Proper nouns must also be capitalized. Unlike common names—general names for people, places, or things, like *person, city, store, school, holiday*—proper nouns are very specific—*Avril Lavigne, Los Angeles, Wal-Mart, Sonora High School, Memorial Day*—and require capitalization to recognize their importance.

Sometimes when we name a person, we need to include a title (*Mr.*, *Rev.*, *Dr.*), abbreviations that follow their name (*Jr.*, *Sr.*, *Esq.*, *Ph.D.*), and initials, for example, **Mr.** Andrew **G.** Milling, **Jr.**, or **Dr.** Nathan **A.** Mahanirananda, **M.D.** As you can see, all three of these items are capitalized.

TIP: Be careful about nouns that can act as either common or proper nouns. For instance, when used alone, the word *president* is a common noun:

The president was an excellent debater and public speaker.

However, when a specific president is named, the title must be capitalized:

President Bush is the forty-third president of the United States.

This rule also applies to family member names as well, *except* when they follow a possessive noun (*Robin's*, *Harold's*, *Marian's*) or a possessive pronoun (*my*, *her*, *his*, *our*, *its*, *their*):

Robin's mother is older than mine.
My dad is taller than me. Mom and Grandma aren't.

North, *south*, *east*, and *west* (the cardinal directions) and the seasons (*spring*, *summer*, *fall*, and *winter*) are not capitalized (except, of course, as the first word in a sentence). When a specific section of the country, like the *Northeast*, is being referred to, or the seasons become part of the title or name of something like *Fall Festival*, *Winter Ball*, or *Spring Fling*, the words are capitalized.

Proper adjectives must be capitalized. A proper adjective is a proper noun acting like an adjective, giving us more information about the person, place, or thing being described. For example, *March winds*, *Italian bread*, and *French toast*.

Finally, when writing a title, remember that the first word, all personal pronouns (*I*, *you*, *he*, *she*, *it*, *they*, *them*, *we*, *us*), all verbs, and all key words in the title are capitalized. Articles (*a*, *an*, and *the*), conjunctions (such as *so*, *for*, *and*, *but*, *nor*, *or*, *yet*), and prepositions of any length (such as *to*, *under*, *beyond*) are not capitalized, however (unless, of course, they are the first word in the title).

TITLES

books	*Number the Stars*
short stories	"The Sound of Summer Running"
newspapers	*The Washington Post*
movies	*Pride and Prejudice*
paintings	*Mona Lisa*
songs	"Jingle Bells"
magazines	*Fortune* magazine

PRACTICE: CAPITALIZATION

Identify and correct all the improperly capitalized words. You can check your answers using the key at the end of the lesson.

1. the statue of liberty is located in new york harbor.

2. "happy birthday, kayla!" jack cheered.

3. playing scrabble is a good way to improve your vocabulary.

4. "place the flowers in the vase," remarked tyneal, "and put them on the front table."

5. pizza and hamburgers were popular choices for the party.

6. dr. seuss's the cat in the hat was played by jim carey in the movie.

7. "what did mom say when you told her you were invited to go to washington, d.c., with teddy?" james asked.

8. juneau is the capital of alaska, our forty-ninth state.

9. subs are called grinders, po' boys, and hoagies in different parts of the united states.

10. grandpa told my uncle that aunt penny and allison went to the grove to go shopping.

ANSWERS

1. The Statue of Liberty is located in New York Harbor.
2. "Happy birthday, Kayla!" Jack cheered.
3. Playing Scrabble is a good way to improve your vocabulary.
4. "Place the flowers in the vase," remarked Tyneal, "and put them on the front table."
5. Pizza and hamburgers were popular choices for the party.
6. Dr. Seuss's The Cat in the Hat was played by Jim Carey in the movie.
7. "What did Mom say when you told her you were invited to go to Washington, D.C., with Teddy?" James asked.
8. Juneau is the capital of Alaska, our forty-ninth state.
9. Subs are called grinders, po' boys, and hoagies in different parts of the United States.
10. Grandpa told my uncle that Aunt Penny and Allison went to The Grove to go shopping.

S E C T I O N 6

confusing words

THE ENGLISH LANGUAGE is filled with confusing words: difficult verbs, words that sound alike but are spelled differently, words that are spelled alike but sound differently, and words and phrases that can contort themselves (what!?). Better word choice is just a few lessons away.

- **Troublesome verbs:** a few irregular verbs are just plain troublesome and need some extra attention.
- **Tricky words:** homonyms and homographs are tricky words that can really throw you for a loop!
- **Misplaced modifiers:** how do you keep those modifiers from *dangling, splitting,* and *squinting*?

troublesome verbs

Words have a longer life than deeds.
PINDAR (522 B.C.–443 B.C.)
GREEK POET

Irregular verbs can be tricky in and of themselves. In this lesson, we will learn about a few that are even more challenging.

WE KNOW THAT irregular verbs don't follow any particular standard form, which can make them troublesome in their own right. There are, though, a few irregular verbs that are exceptionally challenging. Let's look at them.

LAY/LIE

The verb *lay* means to *place* or *put* something somewhere. A noun must follow the verb lay in the sentence.

Present	Present Participle	Past	Past Participle
lay, lays	(am, is, are, was) laying	laid	(have, has) laid

Ursula *laid* the towel on the sand and headed down to the water.

The verb *lie* means to *rest* or *recline* or *be situated*. A noun does not follow the verb *lie* in a sentence, although a prepositional phrase or an adverb may sometimes follow.

Present	Present Participle	Past	Past Participle
lie, lies	(am, is, are, was) lying	lay	(have, has) lain

After her swim, Ursula *lay* on the towel and soaked up the sun.

SET/SIT

Set, like *lay*, means to *place* or *put* something in a particular spot. Also like *lay*, a noun must follow the verb *set* in the sentence.

Present	Present Participle	Past	Past Participle
set, sets	(am, is, are, was) setting	set	(have, has) set

Karla *sets* her rings in the crystal bowl before washing the dishes.

Like *lie*, the verb *sit* means to *be situated*. It can also mean *seated* or *resting*. A noun does not follow the verb *sit* in a sentence, although a prepositional phrase or an adverb may sometimes follow.

Present	Present Participle	Past	Past Participle
sit, sits	(am, is, are, was) sitting	sat	(have, has) sat

Vivian *sits* on the porch to read the newspaper on Saturday mornings.

DID/DONE

Did is the past form of the verb *do*. *Did* is used without a helping verb in a sentence. *Done*, on the other hand, must have a helping verb to be used properly in a sentence.

Incorrect: Paula has did her homework before watching television.

Correct: Paula did her homework before watching television.

Incorrect: Paula done her homework before watching television.

Correct: Paula has done her homework before watching television.

EXCEPT/ACCEPT

Because these two verbs sound so similar, *except* and *accept* are often incorrectly switched in writing (and even in speaking). However, as alike as they sound, their meanings couldn't be more different. *Except* means *apart from* or *excluding*, and *accept* means to *believe* or *willingly receive*.

> *Except* for Tuesdays, I can make plans to meet after school.
>
> I *accept* your apology; thank you.

TIP: Still confused about which to choose—*except* or *accept*? Here's a trick to help you remember. When you are agreeing with someone, you are *accepting* their point of view—you are *cc-eeing* eye to eye with them. When you make an *exception*, you are then *x-cluding* something that you disagree with.

CAN/MAY

Can means *capable of doing something*. When you say, I can lift 250 pounds, you are saying you have the ability to lift that much weight; I can drive a car means that you have the ability to drive a car.

On the other hand, *may* means *having permission to do something*. When you ask, "May I have a piece of cake?" you want to know whether you can have permission to have a piece of cake; when you say, "Ned may come inside now," you are saying Ned has permission to come inside.

> **Incorrect:** Can I get a drink of water?
>
> [Asking if they are *capable* of getting a drink of water, as though something is keeping them from being able to do so.]
>
> **Correct:** May I get a drink of water?
>
> [Asking *permission* to get a drink of water]

TIP: The verbs *hang* and *lie* are tricky because each is both a regular and an irregular verb. Which one it is, and therefore how it is conjugated, depends solely on the context.

If the word *hang* in a sentence means *going to the gallows*, then it is a regular verb, conjugated like this:

Present	Present Participle	Past	Past Participle
hang, hangs	(am, is, are, was) hanging	hanged	(have, has) hanged

On the other hand, if it means *hang out* or *hang a picture on the wall*, then it is an irregular verb, conjugated like this:

Present	Present Participle	Past	Past Participle
hang, hangs	(am, is, are, was) hanging	hung	(have, has) hung

Earlier, we saw that *lie* can mean *to recline*. But it can also mean to *tell an untruth or falsehood*. In this case, you would conjugate it like this:

Present	Present Participle	Past	Past Participle
lie, lies	(am, is, are, was) lying	lied	(have, has) lied

PRACTICE: TROUBLESOME VERBS

Select the correct verb needed to complete each of these sentences. You may check your answers with the key at the end of the chapter.

1. (Can, May) I have some friends over tonight?

2. We would have enjoyed the hike more, (except, accept) Sheila got a blister on her foot.

3. Beatrice (lay, laid) her coat and hat on the chair when she came in.

4. Marcus (has did, has done) a great job keeping up with his chores this summer.

5. How do you expect me to (accept, except) this answer without any explanation?

6. Dad carefully (hanged, hung) the family portrait over the sofa.

7. At the park on a nice day, you can find people (sitting, setting) or (laying, lying) on a blanket relaxing.

8. Jackson, you (can, may) have a second piece of pie if you like.

9. Poor Grandma (has laid, has lain) in bed with a headache most of the afternoon.

10. Without hesitation, the king sentenced the thief to be (hung, hanged) at the gallows.

ANSWERS

1. May
2. except
3. laid
4. has done
5. accept
6. hung
7. sitting, lying
8. may
9. has lain
10. hanged

tricky words

Grammar is a tricky, inconsistent thing. Being the backbone of speech and writing, it should, we think, be eminently logical, make perfect sense, like the human skeleton. But, of course, the skeleton is arbitrary, too. Why twelve pairs of ribs rather than eleven or thirteen? Why thirty-two teeth? It has something to do with evolution and functionalism—but only sometimes, not always. So there are aspects of grammar that make good, logical sense, and others that do not.

JOHN SIMON (1925–   )
CRITIC

Words that sound alike but are spelled differently (**homonyms**), or are spelled the same but pronounced differently (**homographs**) are found all throughout the English language. In this lesson, you will learn many (but not nearly all) of the homonyms and homographs that are out there.

IF YOU'VE EVER looked at a dictionary, you know that there are many tricky words in the English language. We see homonyms and homographs in our reading all of the time, which is proof that it is not only knowing how to spell words correctly that is important, but also knowing *which* word you need to spell in the first place!

HOMONYMS AND HOMOGRAPHS

Words that are pronounced exactly the same, even though they may be spelled differently, are called **homonyms**. The list on the following pages shows you some homonyms we use in our everyday lives.

HOMONYMS

ad/add	The *ad* on the bulletin board was expired.
	Be sure to *add* all of the numbers carefully.
allowed/aloud	I was never *allowed* to ride a motorcycle.
	Reading *aloud* can be fun.
aunt/ant	*Aunt* Rosie is so kind.
	The *ant* carried the leaf across the limb.
ate/eight	Nate *ate* the entire pizza by himself!
	There is enough room for *eight* people in my van.
bear/bare	The brown *bear* lumbered across the field.
	He split the piece of wood with his *bare* hands.
blue/blew	Two *blue* birds chirped in the tree.
	Kelly *blew* the dust off the keyboard.
break/brake	You may have a five-minute *break* now.
	She slammed on the *brake* and went into a skid.
by/buy	Dan and Shelly walked *by* the river.
	You must pay cash when you *buy* gas here.
cent/sent/scent	One *cent* is a penny.
	Omar *sent* his son to his room.
	The *scent* of her perfume was overwhelming.
chews/choose	The puppy *chews* on almost anything.
	You may *choose* the next restaurant.
colonel/kernel	Grandpa was a *colonel* during World War II.
	There was only one *kernel* of popcorn left in the bowl.
deer/dear	Look at the five *deer* beside the house!
	Martha is a *dear* friend.
do/dew/due	*Do* you like this song?
	I could see the morning *dew* on the grass.
	My report is *due* in two days.
ewe/you/yew	The *ewe* watched her lamb from afar.
	You are my best friend.
	A *yew* is a small evergreen.
flew/flu/flue	The plane *flew* high overhead.
	She gets a vaccination for the *flu* each year.
	He forgot to open the *flue* in the chimney.
flour/flower	*Flour* is needed to make bread.
	The pink *flower* looked pretty in the window.

HOMONYMS *(Continued)*

he'll/heal/heel	*He'll* be going to college next year.
	Will your scratch *heal* soon?
	My *heel* hurt for three days after the fall.
here/hear	Please place the paper *here* on the desk.
	Grandma doesn't *hear* well.
hole/whole	The dog dug a *hole* by the backyard fence.
	She ate the apple *whole* instead of slicing it.
hour/our	It was a ten-*hour* drive to Virginia.
	Our house needs new shutters.
I'll/aisle/isle	*I'll* be leaving soon.
	She pushed the cart down the *aisle*.
	The small *isle* off the coast was uninhabited.
knew/new	I *knew* I should have chosen the green one.
	My *new* shoes hurt my feet.
knot/not	It was impossible to get the *knot* out of her shoestring.
	Jason would *not* say he was sorry.
know/no	Do you *know* the capital of New Jersey?
	No way!
meet/meat	The track *meet* was this weekend.
	The *meat* is in the freezer.
need/kneed/knead	You will *need* one stick of butter for that recipe.
	The midfielder got *kneed* in the leg by his opponent.
	The recipe said to *knead* the dough after it raised.
one/won	*One* slice of pizza remained in the pan.
	Cory was glad that he *won* the prize.
pair/pear	Wash this *pair* of jeans before wearing them.
	The *pear* was ripe and juicy.
principal/principle	My *principal* was a kind man.
	Paul was a man of *principle*.
rain/rein/reign	It might *rain* tomorrow afternoon.
	Take hold of the horse's *rein* and pull back gently.
	The king's *reign* was successful for 30 years.
right/write/rite	I like to be *right*.
	It's important to learn to *write* well.
	Marriage is a *rite* of passage.

HOMONYMS *(Continued)*

sail/sale	Mrs. Williman likes to *sail* with her family.
	This sofa was on *sale*.
scene/seen	The winter *scene* was almost surreal.
	Have you ever *seen* a three-toed sloth?
there/their/they're	*There* are probably a million ants here!
	Has *their* team won many games?
	I think that *they're* twins.
threw/through	The center fielder *threw* the ball to third to make the out.
	Red Ridinghood walked *through* the forest to Grandma's house.
to/too/two	*To* lock the door, just turn the key.
	I have had to tell him *too* often to turn his music down.
	The *two* rolls left in the bag were moldy.
wood/would	Chopping *wood* is hard work.
	I *would* like to order a steamed lobster, please.
which/witch	Tony didn't know *which* movie to see first.
	The Good *Witch* of the North was kinder than her sister.
weather/whether	The *weather* turned frigid overnight.
	Harold had to decide *whether* he wanted to leave early.
whose/who's	*Whose* muddy shoes are these?
	I don't know *who's* supposed to be going with us.

Homographs are words that are spelled exactly the same way, but have completely different meanings. The following list shows some familiar homographs.

HOMOGRAPHS

address	*Address* the envelope in script. The *address* is on the desk.
	address: directions for delivery
	address: place where a business or person resides
bass	The professional *bass* fisherman also plays *bass* in a band.
	bass: a type of freshwater fish *bass:* a stringed instrument
bow	He will *bow* before the king and present him with a golden *bow*.
	bow: to bend at the waist
	bow: flexible wood used for shooting arrows

HOMOGRAPHS *(Continued)*

close	The store owner lives *close* to the store. He'll *close* up tonight. *close:* to be near in proximity *close:* to shut
conflict	The stories' details *conflict* about the country's initial *conflict*. *conflict:* to disagree *conflict:* a disagreement
desert	It was easy to *desert* his town in the *desert* for the city life. *desert:* to leave *desert:* a barren, dry place
does	*Does* the ranger see the whitetail *does* down by the stream? *does:* interrogative (questioning verb) *does:* more than one female deer
dove	The *dove* angrily *dove* in the flock of gulls to defend his mate. *dove:* a white bird d*ove:* past tense of the verb dive
house	This duplex *house* can *house* more than one family. *house:* a place to live *house:* to contain or to shelter
lead	While in the *lead*, the contestant's *lead* broke in both pencils. *lead:* at the head or front position *lead:* graphite metal substance used in pencils
live	The stadium I *live* next to has many *live* concerts. *live:* to reside *live:* not pre-recorded or taped
minute	At one *minute* after midnight, the *minute* creature disappeared. *minute:* one-sixtieth of an hour *minute:* very small
present	It was an honor to *present* this special *present* to the king. *present:* to give *present:* a gift
produce	Local growers *produce produce* to sell all summer long. *produce:* to create, to grow, or to generate *produce:* vegetables and fruit
read	Although I've *read* the book before, I will gladly *read* it again. *read:* past tense of the verb read *read:* to examine and understand the meanings of written words
record	The school will officially *record* this newly defeated *record*. *record:* to write, to register, or to document something *record:* a list of achievements
separate	Use *separate* files to *separate* this year's work from last year's. *separate:* disconnected *separate:* to keep apart
tear	A *tear* came to her eye when she saw him *tear* the note in two. *tear:* watery, saline fluid that is released from the eyes *tear:* to rip

HOMOGRAPHS *(Continued)*

use	If you don't have any *use* for this basket, may I *use* it? *use:* the need to use *use:* to take or to consume
well	*Well,* we sent her home because she didn't feel *well.* *well:* an interjection used to introduce a thought *well:* good or satisfactory health
wind	I tried to *wind* the kite string but the strong *wind* pulled it away. *wind:* to wrap around or coil *wind:* air velocity or movement
wound	He *wound* the bandage around his *wound* to protect it. *wound:* wrapped around *wound:* a minor injury

PRACTICE: HOMONYMS AND HOMOGRAPHS

Look at each set of clues to determine the words that they are describing. Then identify whether those words homonyms or homographs. You may use the word bank on the previous pages to help you. Check your answers in the section that follows.

1. to bend at the waist *or* a large tree branch: HOMONYM / HOMOGRAPH

2. correct *or* a sacrament *or* to jot down: HOMONYM / HOMOGRAPH

3. devoured *or* ten minus two: HOMONYM / HOMOGRAPH

4. discounted price *or* to navigate a small boat: HOMONYM / HOMOGRAPH

5. permitted to do something *or* easy to hear: HOMONYM / HOMOGRAPH

6. tiny *or* sixty seconds: HOMONYM / HOMOGRAPH

7. motionless *or* fancy writing paper: HOMONYM / HOMOGRAPH

8. uppercase (letter) *or* center of state government: HOMONYM / HOMOGRAPH

9. to make something *or* fresh fruits and vegetables: HOMONYM / HOMOGRAPH

10. to move quickly through the air *or* a pesky insect: HOMONYM / HOMOGRAPH

11. gnaws *or* decide on: HOMONYM / HOMOGRAPH

12. a freshwater fish *or* a low-toned voice or guitar: HOMONYM / HOMOGRAPH

13. excessively *or* deuce: HOMONYM / HOMOGRAPH

14. aroma *or* dispatched: HOMONYM / HOMOGRAPH

15. nearby *or* to secure: HOMONYM / HOMOGRAPH

ANSWERS

1. bow *or* bough: HOMONYM
2. right *or* rite *or* write: HOMONYM
3. ate *or* eight: HOMONYM
4. sale *or* sail: HOMONYM
5. allowed *or* aloud: HOMONYM
6. minute *or* minute: HOMOGRAPH
7. stationary *or* stationery: HOMONYM
8. capital *or* capitol: HOMONYM
9. produce *or* produce: HOMOGRAPH
10. fly *or* fly : HOMOGRAPH
11. chews *or* choose: HOMONYM
12. bass *or* bass: HOMOGRAPH
13. too *or* two: HOMONYM
14. scent *or* sent: HOMONYM
15. close *or* close: HOMOGRAPH

misplaced modifiers

*Grammar and logic free language from being
at the mercy of the tone of voice. Grammar protects us
against misunderstanding the sound of an uttered name;
logic protects us against what we say having double meaning.*
EUGENE ROSENSTOCK HUESSY (1888–1973)
SOCIOLOGIST AND PHILOSOPHER

Dangling, split, and squinting modifiers can wreak havoc on your writing (and maybe even make you laugh). In this lesson, you will learn how to steer clear of these modifying mistakes.

MODIFIERS ENHANCE A sentence. These enhancers include adjectives and adverbs, as well as phrases and clauses that behave like adjectives and adverbs. Without modifiers, our sentences would be uninteresting and dull. Modifiers can make written and spoken language more interesting and meaningful, and easier to understand.

Sometimes, even though modifiers are helpful, they can become **misplaced** and confuse the reader or listener. It happens more often than you think.

What do misplaced modifiers look like? Read on to find out.

DANGLING MODIFIERS

Just like adverbs and adjectives, phrases that function like adjectives or adverbs should be put near the words they are modifying to avoid confusion. You want to avoid a **dangling modifier**.

Ben's grandpa mowed the lawn *wearing a bright red hat.*

Who is wearing the bright red hat—Grandpa or the lawn?

A better way to word the sentence would be to move the modifying participial phrase closer to *Ben's grandpa*, which is the noun it's enhancing.

Wearing a bright red hat, Ben's grandpa mowed the lawn.

SQUINTING MODIFIERS

When a modifier is vague, appearing to describe the nouns on both sides of it, it is called a **squinting modifier**. For instance:

Brushing your teeth *frequently* helps keep cavities away.

Does this mean you should brush your teeth frequently in order to keep cavities away?

Frequently brushing your teeth helps keep cavities away.

Or does it mean that brushing your teeth can frequently help keep cavities away?

Frequently, brushing your teeth helps keep cavities away.

SPLIT INFINITIVES

As we learned in Lesson 3, the infinitive form of a verb begins with the word *to*, for example, *to play, to dance,* or *to study.* Inserting a word or phrase between *to* and the verb creates a **split infinitive**, disrupting the flow of the sentence.

Incorrect: The team was told to, before the game, warm up by running around the field.

Correct: The team was told to warm up by running around the field before the game.

OR

Before the game, the team was told to warm up by running around the field.

MANAGING MODIFIERS

Whenever possible, place simple adjectives before the nouns they are modifying.

Sporting a *new football* jersey, the *excited* fan stood in the rain for hours to buy a ticket to the *big* game.

Place any phrases and clauses acting as adjectives as near as possible to the noun being modified.

The dog *with brown and white spots* wagged its tail happily.

Strategically placing limiting modifiers like *only, barely, just,* and *almost* can widely vary a sentence's meaning.

Only John plays baseball.	[No one else can play it, only John.]
John *only* plays baseball.	[He doesn't watch it or read about it; he only plays it.]
John plays baseball *only*.	[He doesn't play anything else but baseball.]

PRACTICE: MISPLACED MODIFIERS

Rewrite each of these sentences so that the modifier is correctly placed. Check your answers on the following page.

1. While riding my bike to the library, the dog began to bark.

2. She observed the monstrous skyscraper with binoculars.

3. Donna served hot dogs, fries, and potato salad to her guests on paper plates.

4. Did you see a guy cross the bridge with a beard?

5. The red sports car was reported stolen by the police officer.

6. While fixing my bicycle chain, the ice cream man drove by.

7. Buddy sat in the chair with a broken leg.

8. Sam played the "Star-Spangled Banner" to the audience on his saxophone.

9. Covered with dirt, I saw the farmer plowing his field on my bike.

10. While lacing my shoelaces, the cat yawned and settled into the chair.

ANSWERS

1. While I was riding my bike to the library, the dog began to bark.
2. With binoculars, she observed the monstrous skyscraper.
3. Donna served hot dogs, fries, and potato salad on paper plates to her guests.
4. Did you see a guy with a beard cross the bridge?
5. The stolen red sports car was reported by the police officer.
6. The ice cream man drove by while I was fixing my bicycle chain.
7. Buddy, who had a broken leg, sat in the chair.
8. Sam played the "Star-Spangled Banner" on his saxophone to the audience.
9. While on my bike, I saw the farmer who was covered with dirt plowing his field.
10. While I was lacing my shoelaces, the cat yawned and settled into the chair.

POSTTEST

NOW THAT YOU have completed 30 lessons in grammar, it's time to find out how much you've improved! The posttest that follows includes 30 questions based on the grammar concepts you've just learned. To check yourself, go to page 204 for the answers. It is suggested that you write your answers to the posttest on a separate piece of paper so you can review and test yourself as many times as you need.

POSTTEST

1. (Circle) the common nouns, underline the proper nouns, and [box] the abstract nouns.

Missouri	laziness	pride
glass	jewelry	Peru
horizon	toast	glue
evil	integrity	dessert
drawing	loneliness	canoe
juice	fear	pennies

2. Underline the antecedents/pronouns that properly agree in gender.

Ben / it	Mr. Hoyle / they
knives / they	Chelsea / she
rice / they	man / him

3. Underline the antecedents/pronouns that agree in number.

mice / they	band / they	lion / it
moose / they	moose / it	fish / it
some / he or she	group / we	some / they

4. Underline the action verbs.

serve	did	blew	cook
give	are	spoke	chased
look	could	rest	fry

5. Underline the linking verbs.

proved	took	grew	sat
became	appear	could	nodded
felt	tastes	is	dust

6. [Box] the regular verbs and underline the irregular verbs.

hug	climb	hold	choose
cross	cost	fly	save
buy	make	read	sting

7. Circle the correct form of *lay/lie* in each sentence.

The old haunted house (lays, lies) across the river.

We have (lain, laid) out our uniforms for the game.

Who (laid, lain) the TV remote on the floor?

8. Circle the correct form of *sit/set* in each sentence.

The waitress (set, sat) the ketchup bottles on the table.

We will (sit, set) beside the bleachers in our own chairs.

Mom (set, sat) down on the bench to watch Gina and Greg play in the playground.

9. Identify the tense of the verbs that follow as present, past, future, present perfect, past perfect, future perfect, present progressive, past progressive, or future progressive.

will buy _____   am buying _____

will mow _____   mow _____

had bought _____   have bought _____

has mown _____   will have mown _____

10. Circle the common adjectives in these sentences.

My next-door neighbor's dog darted across the front yard chasing the red ball.

The chorus teacher, Mrs. Johnson, has a very melodious voice.

The sweet smell of jasmine filled the air when the tree bloomed.

11. Write the correct indefinite pronoun in front of each noun.

___ loaf   ___ umbrella   ___ honest person

___ universal truth   ___ needle and thread   ___ shopkeeper

___ one-way street   ___ only child   ___ apple

___ chair   ___ elegant lady   ___ historian

___ mythical creature   ___ queue   ___ insult

12. Change the following proper nouns into proper adjectives by crossing out and writing in what's needed.

Jamaica   California   Germany

China   Mexico   Alaska

Italy   Georgia   Maya

13. Determine whether each **boldfaced** word in the sentences is a possessive pronoun or a possessive adjective by writing PP or PA above it.

My little sister Joanne says that it's not **her** fault, it's **mine**.

Kyle's mom let **him** and Dan go to the mall to buy a present for **their** father.

"This one's **his**; that one's **yours**," Vin counted, "and those three are **theirs**."

14. Determine whether each **boldfaced** word in the sentences is a demonstrative pronoun or a demonstrative adjective by writing DP or DA above it.

What was the title of **that** movie we saw last weekend?

Those have got to be the funniest pictures I've ever seen!

I will have to take **this** suit to the dry cleaners to get **these** spots out.

15. (Circle) the form of the adjective (positive, comparative, or superlative) that best completes each sentence.

The weather today was (bad, worse) than yesterday's.

The (longer, longest) the wait, the (most, more) it irritates Grandpa.

It was the (most interesting, interestinger) conversation I've had with her yet.

16. (Circle) the correct form of the adverb (positive, comparative, or superlative) in these sentences.

Matthew (more frequently, most frequently) does his homework on the kitchen table.

Our team played the (bestest, best) of all the teams at the tournament.

This presentation is going (slowly, more slowly) than I thought it would.

17. <u>Underline</u> the adjectives and [box] the adverbs in these sentences.

The spotted yellow-and-black butterfly fluttered happily around the yard.

Pamela often jogged around the neighborhood park after work to unwind.

Natalie watched closely as Rhonda carefully poured the thick black paint into the small plastic bottle.

18. <u>Underline</u> the prepositional phrases in the sentences below.

While the horse ate in the stable, the cow and the goat grazed lazily in the field.

Arpan quickly drank from his thermos before the second half of the game started.

Our fish, Bubba, always seems lonely in his small fish tank.

19. Rewrite each sentence so that the misplaced modifiers are properly placed.

The culprit was described as a short man with a dark beard weighing 137 pounds.

_____

They visited the college wearing varsity jackets.

_____

Smothered in barbecue sauce, we devoured the platter of ribs.

_____

20. <u>Underline</u> the simple subjects and [box] the simple predicates.

Many people visit the Statue of Liberty every year.

The phone rang six times before I could answer it.

What is the sum of the numbers twelve and eleven?

21. Identify whether the **boldfaced** word is a direct or an indirect object in these sentences by writing DO or IO above it.

I would like peach **ice cream** with my peach cobbler, please.

The postman delivered **Aunt Martha** a **package** today.

The class sent the **soldiers** several **care packages**.

22. ⟨Circle⟩ the verb that correctly agrees with the subject in each sentence.

They (studies, study) together every Wednesday night.

My neighbor's dog (bark, barks) a lot at night.

Spaghetti and meatballs (is, are) my favorite Italian meal.

23. ⟨Circle⟩ the verb that will agree with the indefinite pronouns in the following sentences.

Alice is right; only a few of us (likes, like) split pea soup.

Each of the students (are, is) receiving an award.

None of the teachers (give, gives) homework over the holidays.

24. Determine which pronoun best fits for proper pronoun–antecedent agreement in these sentences.

Either Troy or Marty will bring _____ camera to take pictures at the parade.

Marge never lets _____ cat outside.

Tina and Patricia started _____ tennis lesson today.

25. Correctly identify the types of phrases in the sentences below.

Betsy, *who tried to avoid slipping on the ice*, wore her winter boots.

a. participial phrase   **b.** appositive phrase   **c.** gerund phrase

Washing windows on a skyscraper can be a scary job.

a. participial phrase   **b.** appositive phrase   **c.** gerund phrase

Sitting in the sun, the cat dozed contentedly.

a. participial phrase   **b.** appositive phrase   **c.** gerund phrase

26. Determine whether the group of words is an independent or a subordinate clause by writing IC or SC.

Mr. Christopher teaches English ____   If it rains tomorrow ____

Although you might change
your mind ____   We'll see ___

Please pass the butter ____   When we got to the shore ____

27. Identify the coordinating conjunction in each sentence and <u>underline</u> the word or group of words it is connecting.

    The lemonade was cold and delicious.

    The little piano etude was simple yet lovely.

    Jared did not like the movie, nor did Walter.

28. Identify the simple, compound, complex, and compound-complex sentences.
    a. Shelly raked the leaves and placed them into the compost pile.
    b. On Saturday mornings, I enjoy orange juice with my pancakes.
    c. I like chocolate-covered almonds and cashews.
    d. When the weather is cold, Dad likes to build a fire and read a favorite book.

29. Add punctuation where necessary in the following items.

    Campers could play tennis soccer basketball or baseball

    What kind of day did I have The hamster got loose in the house the washing machine overflowed and Jimmy fell and skinned both knees

    Wow This project is terrific

30. Correctly place quotation marks, commas, and endmarks in these sentences.

    You should close the windows and lock them before going to bed suggested Ian

    Matt blurted Hey That's my bowl of popcorn Get your own

    Why interrupted Mrs. Ross do you always insist on sitting in the front seat

ANSWERS

1. Common nouns: glass, horizon, drawing, juice, jewelry, toast, glue, dessert, canoe, pennies; proper nouns: Missouri, Peru; abstract nouns: evil, laziness, integrity, loneliness, fear, pride.
2. knives / they, Chelsea / she, man / him
3. mice / they, lion / it, moose / they, moose / it, fish / it, some / he or she, some / they
4. serve, did, blew, cook, give, spoke, chased, look, rest, fry
5. proved, grew, became, appear, felt, tastes, is
6. Regular verbs: hug, cross, climb, save; irregular verbs: buy, cost, make, hold, fly, read, choose, sting
7. lies, laid, laid
8. set, sit, sat
9. will buy = future   will mow = future
   had bought = past perfect   has mown = present perfect
   am buying = present progressive   mow = present
   have bought = present perfect   will have mown = future perfect
10. next-door, front, red, chorus, melodious, sweet
11. a loaf   an umbrella   an honest person
    a universal truth   a needle and thread   a shopkeeper
    a one-way street   an only child   an apple
    a chair   an elegant lady   a historian
    a mythical creature   a queue   an insult
12. Jamaican, Californian, German, Chinese, Mexican, Alaskan, Italian, Georgian, Mayan
13. PP = possessive pronoun, PA = possessive adjective
    My = PA, her = PA, mine = PP
    him = PP, their = PA
    his = PP, yours = PP, theirs = PP
14. DP = demonstrative pronoun, DA = demonstrative adjective
    that = DA, those = DP, this = DA, these = DA
15. worse, longer, more, most interesting
16. most frequently, best, more slowly
17. The <u>spotted</u> <u>yellow-and-black</u> butterfly fluttered ⬚happily⬚ around the yard.

    Pamela ⬚often⬚ jogged around the <u>neighborhood</u> park after work to unwind.

    Natalie watched ⬚closely⬚ as Rhonda ⬚carefully⬚ poured the <u>thick</u> <u>black</u> paint into the <u>small</u> <u>plastic</u> bottle.

18. While the horse ate <u>in the stable</u>, the cow and the goat grazed lazily <u>in the field</u>.

Arpan quickly drank <u>from his thermos</u> before the second half <u>of the game</u> started.

Our fish, Bubba, always seems lonely <u>in his small fish tank</u>.

19. (possible answers)

The culprit was described as a short man weighing 137 pounds with a dark beard.

Wearing their varsity jackets, they visited the college.

We devoured the platter of ribs that were smothered in barbecue sauce.

20. Many <u>people</u> $\boxed{\text{visit}}$ the Statue of Liberty every year.

The <u>phone</u> $\boxed{\text{rang}}$ six times before I could answer it.

What $\boxed{\text{is}}$ the <u>sum</u> of the numbers twelve and eleven?

21. DO = direct object, IO = indirect object

ice cream = DO, Aunt Martha = IO, package = DO, soldiers = IO, care package = DO

22. study, barks, is

23. like, is, give

24. his, her, their

25. **b.** appositive phrase, **c.** gerund phrase, **a.** participial phrase

26. IC = independent clause, SC = subordinate clause

Mr. Christopher teaches English = IC

If it rains tomorrow = SC

Although you might change your mind = SC

We'll see = IC

Please pass the butter = IC

When we got to the shore = SC

27. The lemonade was <u>cold</u> **and** <u>delicious</u>.

The little piano etude was <u>simple</u> **yet** <u>lovely</u>.

<u>Jared</u> did not like the movie, **nor** did <u>Walter</u>.

28. (a) compound, (b) complex, (c) simple, (d) compound-complex

29. Campers could play tennis, soccer, basketball, or baseball.

What kind of day did I have? The hamster got loose in the house, the washing machine overflowed, and Jimmy fell and skinned both knees.

Wow! This project is terrific!

30. "You should close the windows and lock them before going to bed," suggested Ian.

Matt blurted, "Hey! That's my bowl of popcorn! Get your own!"

"Why," interrupted Mrs. Ross, "do you always insist on sitting in the front seat?"

hints for taking standardized tests

THE TERM *standardized test* has the ability to produce fear in test takers. These tests are often given by a state board of education or a nationally recognized education group. Usually these tests are taken in the hope of getting accepted—whether it's for a special program, the next grade in school, or even to a college or university. Here's the good news: Standardized tests are more familiar to you than you know. In most cases, these tests look very similar to tests that your teachers may have given in the classroom.

The following pages include valuable tips for combating test anxiety—that sinking or blank feeling some people feel as they begin a test or encounter a difficult question. You'll discover how to use your time wisely and how to avoid errors when you're taking a test. Also, you will find a plan for preparing for the test and for the test day. Once you have these tips down, you're ready to approach any exam head-on!

COMBATING TEST ANXIETY

Take the Test One Question at a Time

Focus all your attention on the question you're answering. Block out any thoughts about questions you've already read or concerns about what's coming next. Concentrate your thinking where it will do the most good—on the present question.

If You Lose Your Concentration

Don't worry about it! It's normal. During a long test, it happens to everyone. When your mind is stressed, it takes a break whether you want it to or not. It's easy to get your concentration back if you simply acknowledge the fact that you've lost it and take a quick break.

If You Freeze before or during the Test

Don't worry about a question that stumps you. Mark it and go on to the next question. You can come back to the "stumper" later. Try to put it out of your mind completely until you come back to it. Chances are, the memory block will be gone by the time you return to the question.

If you freeze before you even begin the test, here's what to do:

1. Take a little time to look over the test.
2. Read a few of the questions.
3. Decide which are the easiest and start there.
4. Before long, you'll be "in the groove."

TIME STRATEGIES

With the strategies in this section, you'll notice the next timed test you take is not as scary.

Pace Yourself

The most important time strategy is pacing yourself. Before you begin, take just a few seconds to survey the test, noting the number of questions and the sections that look easier than the rest. Estimate a time schedule based upon the amount of time available to you. Mark the halfway point on your test and make a note beside that mark of what the time will be when the testing period is half over.

Keep Moving

Once you begin the test, keep moving. If you work slowly in an attempt to make fewer mistakes, your mind will become bored and begin to wander, and you will lose concentration.

The Process of Elimination

For some standardized tests, there is no guessing penalty. What this means is that you shouldn't be afraid to guess. For a multiple-choice question with four answer choices, you have a one in four chance of guessing correctly. And your chances improve if you can eliminate a choice or two.

By using the process of elimination, you will cross out incorrect answer choices and improve your odds of finding the correct answer. In order for the process of elimination to work, you must keep track of what choices you are crossing out. Cross out incorrect choices on the test booklet itself. If you don't cross out an incorrect answer, you may still think it is a possible answer. Crossing out any incorrect answers makes it easier to identify the right answer: There will be fewer places where it can hide!

AVOIDING ERRORS

When you take a test, you want to make as few errors as possible in the questions you answer. Here are a few tactics to keep in mind.

Control Yourself

If you feel rushed or worried, stop for a few seconds. Acknowledging the feeling (*Hmmm! I'm feeling a little pressure here!*), take a few deep breaths, and send yourself a few positive messages (*I am prepared for this test, and I will do well!*).

Directions

In many standardized testing situations, specific instructions are given and you must follow them as best as you can. Be sure you understand what is expected. If you don't, ask. Listen carefully for instructions about how to answer the questions and make certain you know how much time you have to complete the task. If you miss any important information about the rules of taking the test, **ask for it**.

If You Finish Early

Use any time you have left at the end of the test or test section to check your work. First, make sure you've put the right answers in the right places. After you've checked for errors, take a second look at the more difficult questions. If you have a good reason for thinking your first response was wrong, change it.

THE DAYS BEFORE THE TEST

Physical Activity

Get some exercise in the days preceding the test. Play a game outside with your friends or take your pet for a walk. Exercise helps give more oxygen to your brain and allows your thinking performance to rise on the day you take the test. But moderation is key here. You don't want to exercise so much that you feel too tired; however, a little physical activity will do the trick.

Balanced Diet

Like your body, your brain needs the proper nutrients to function well. Eat plenty of fruits and vegetables in the days before the test. Foods like fish and beans are also good choices to help your mind reach its best level of performance before a big test.

Rest

Get plenty of sleep the nights before the test. Go to bed at a reasonable time, and you'll feel relaxed and rested.

TEST DAY

It's finally here: the day of the big test! Eat a good breakfast, and avoid anything high in sugar (even though it might taste good, no sugary cereal or doughnuts). If you can, get to your classroom early so you can review your materials before the test begins. The best thing to do next is to relax and think positively! Before you know it, the test will be over, and you'll walk away knowing you did the best job you could!

GLOSSARY

abstract noun   a word denoting something that cannot be seen or touched, such as *freedom* or *pride*.

action verb   a physical or mental verb.

adjective   a word that modifies a noun or pronoun. Adjectives answer *what kind? which one? how much? how many?* about a noun or pronoun.

adverb   a word that modifies a verb, an adjective, or another adverb. Adverbs answer *where? when? how much? how many?* about the verb, adjective, or other adverb.

antecedent   the word or words to which a specific pronoun refers.

appositive phrase   a word or phrase that identifies the noun or pronoun that comes before it in the sentence.

clause   a group of words with a subject and a verb.

collective noun   a word that names groups of living things.

colon   the punctuation mark that comes before a series, a lengthy quotation, or an example, or after the salutation in a business letter.

comma   the punctuation mark that is used to separate words, phrases, and items in a series.

common noun   ordinary name for a person, place, or thing.

complex sentence   a sentence that is made up of an independent clause and subordinate (dependent) clause.

compound-complex sentence   a sentence that is made up of more than one independent clause and at least one subordinate clause.

compound noun   a new noun made up of two or more single nouns. Compound nouns may be fused (spelled as one word), hyphenated, or spelled as two separate words.

compound sentence   a sentence that contains at least two independent clauses with no subordinate (dependent) clauses.

compound subject   two or more subjects that share the same verb in a sentence.

concrete noun   a word denoting things that are countable and uncountable.

conjunction   a word or phrase that connect other words or groups of words.

dangling modifier   a word or phrase that is meant to modify one specific component in the sentence, but because of poor placement, alters the meaning of the sentence.

dash   the punctuation mark that indicates a strong pause to emphasize a point, or to set off a comment or a short list within a sentence.

demonstrative pronoun   the words *this, that, these,* and *those,* used to replace a specific noun in a sentence.

direct object   a noun or pronoun that receives the action of the verb.

direct quotation   the exact spoken or written words of a person written by another; they must be enclosed in quotation marks.

endmarks   punctuation marks that belong at the end of a sentence.

exclamation point   the punctuation mark that is used to indicate strong emotion in writing.

first-person pronoun   the pronouns *I, my, mine, me, myself, we, our, ours, us, ourselves.*

fragment   an incomplete sentence that lacks either a subject or a predicate.

future tense   the verb tense that implies that something hasn't yet happened, but will.

gerund phrase   a phrase that begins with an *-ing* verb and functions as a noun in a sentence.

homograph   one of two words that are spelled exactly the same way, but have completely different meanings.

homonym   one of two distinct words that have different spellings and meanings but are pronounced the same way.

hyphen   the punctuation mark that is used to join or separate numbers, letters, syllables, and words for specific purposes.

indefinite pronoun   a word that refers to a noun, but not a specific one, such as *no one*, *anyone*, *anybody*, or *somebody*.

independent clause   a group of words that contain a subject and a predicate (verb) and can stand by itself as a sentence.

infinitive phrase   a phrase beginning with the infinitive form of a verb (it follows the word *to*) that functions as a noun, an adjective, or an adverb in a sentence.

irregular verb   a verb that does not use an *-ed* ending in the past tense. The past tense endings for irregular verbs do not follow any specific pattern.

italicizing   a way of showing *emphasis* of a word or words in a sentence or to distinguish them from other words in the text, such as with titles.

linking verb   a state-of-being or condition verb that links a noun with either another noun or an adjective.

misplaced modifier   a word or phrase that is placed too far from something it is modifying, but does not alter the meaning of the sentence or require further clarification.

modifier   a word that modifies, or changes, another word. Adjectives modify only nouns. Adverbs modify verbs, adjectives, and other adverbs.

noun   a word that names a person, place, or thing (including ideas and feelings).

object of the preposition   the noun or pronoun that follows a phrase that begins with a preposition; often abbreviated *OOP*.

object pronoun   a pronoun that is the object of the sentence (the person or thing receiving the action from the verb).

parentheses   the punctuation marks that are used to set off information that is not necessarily pertinent to the surrounding sentence or words.

participial phrase   a phrase that begins with an *-ing* word and functions as an adjective in a sentence.

past tense   the verb tense that implies something that already happened.

perfect tense   the verb tense that implies that an event or state was started and ended.

period   the punctuation mark found at the end of a declarative sentence, an imperative sentence, an indirect question, and in abbreviations.

personal pronouns   words such as *I, you, me, he, him, she, her, it, they, them,* and *we* that refer to the speaker, the person or thing being spoken about, or the person or thing being spoken to.

phrase   a group of words that do not have a subject and verb. Phrases can act like various parts of speech (noun, verb, adjective, adverb, or preposition).

predicate   another word for *verb*.

preposition   a word which shows the relationship of a noun or pronoun to another word in the sentence in terms of time and/or space.

prepositional phrase   a phrase beginning with a preposition and ending with a noun or pronoun.

present tense   the verb tense that implies action happening in the present or an action which happens constantly.

pronoun   a word that takes the place of a noun in a sentence. A pronoun can be possessive, demonstrative, personal, and indefinite.

proper noun   a very specific noun which is indicated by its capitalization.

punctuation   a set of special symbols that imply specific directions for the reader to better understand the writer's meaning.

question mark   the punctuation mark placed at the end of an interrogatory sentence (a question).

quotation marks   the punctuation marks used to indicate the exact words of a speaker or to convey hesitation or misgiving in a person's written words.

run-on   a sentence that consists of two or more sentences combined improperly without proper punctuation.

second-person pronoun   the pronouns *you, your, yours, yourself, yourselves.*

semicolon   the punctuation mark used to join together two independent clauses that share a similar idea and are not already joined by a conjunction.

sentence   a group of words that share a subject and predicate, and express a complete thought.

sentence fragment   an incomplete thought punctuated as a complete sentence.

simple sentence   an independent clause.

subject-verb agreement   when the subject and the verb of a sentence agree in number and in person.

subordinate clause   (a.k.a., dependent clause) a group of words that includes a subject and a verb, but cannot stand alone as a complete thought.

superlative   the form of an adjective or adverb that implies the greatest degree compared to that of something else. Superlatives end in the suffix *-est*.

third-person pronouns   the pronouns *he, his, him, himself, she, her, hers, herself, it, its, itself, they, their, theirs, them, themselves.*

underlining   a way of showing <u>emphasis</u> of a word or words in a sentence or to distinguish them from other words in the text, such as with titles.

verb   a word that expresses action or condition of the corresponding noun or pronoun. Verbs can also indicate the time of the action or condition.

NOTES

NOTES

NOTES

NOTES

NOTES

NOTES